Better Homes and Gardens.

tiling

Step-by-Step

Meredith® Books
Des Moines, Iowa

TABLE OF CONTENTS

Planning
YOUR TILING PROJECT 8

Tile
PROJECTS 32

Tools
AND MATERIALS 108

Tiling
TECHNIQUES 128

Maintenance
AND REPAIR 146

INTRODUCTION

Many people think they must hire a professional contractor to install ceramic tile. They assume it takes years of practice and on-the-job experience to tile. Years ago, tiling installations demanded the keen eye and practiced hand of a professional, but today new materials and techniques make tiling easier for a do-it-yourselfer to handle. Tile installation still requires patience and some basic do-it-yourself construction skills, but with the right information, proper tools, and correct materials, homeowners can achieve a professional-looking job on their own.

Step-by-Step Tiling Projects provides the information you need to plan and carry out a tiling job. You will learn how to plan the project, how to decide which types of tile to use in different installations, what types of adhesives to choose and how to use them, and how to finish and maintain your project so it will provide you with years of service.

Step-by-Step Tiling Projects will help you decide which jobs you can take on yourself. Even if you decide not to do the job yourself, you will be better equipped to manage the job wisely: Tiling professionals appreciate working with an educated client. If you choose to hire out the job, you will be better equipped to find the right contractor, choose the right materials, and achieve the results you want.

How to use this book
Begin by reading the first chapter, "Planning Your Tiling Project." It provides a gallery of tile designs, followed by descriptions of the many types of tile available and the pros and cons of using tile in various locations. Using this knowledge you will be better able to determine whether the project you have in mind makes sense.

Once you know what you want, the next step is to gain an understanding of how to get it. "Tile Projects" presents a series of specific tile installations, including the information and guidance you need to complete each one. This section also will help you determine the feasibility of tiling plans and assess whether you feel you have the skills to do the job yourself.

"Tools and Materials" gives you all the basic information you need to select the tools, as well as the materials— including the tiles themselves—you need to turn your ideas into reality.

Read the chapter "Tiling Techniques" from beginning to end before you start any work. There you will receive a brief apprenticeship in tile setting. You'll learn some basic tool skills and gain an understanding of each of the steps necessary for your tiling project.

Finally "Maintenance and Repair" offers proven tips to make old tile installations look new again and to ensure that a new installation doesn't age prematurely.

Tip boxes
In addition to the basic instructions, "You'll Need" boxes tell you up front what time, skills, and tools each project requires. Pay special attention to the "Caution" boxes: They warn you to watch out for dangerous situations and help keep you from doing damage to yourself or the job at hand.

Other information boxes provide helpful hints, such as how to take accurate measurements, how to cut costs by accurately estimating material needs, and how to organize a job to minimize wasted labor. Others provide tricks of the trade to help you do a job quickly and easily.

MURAL BACKSPLASH

What might have been a plain kitchen backsplash has become the focal point of the space with the addition of a decorative mural. A decorative mural is a great way to establish the "theme" of your home. And, in this case, using the water-resistant tiles will protect the walls from water damage and other stains. See page 66 for step-by-step instructions on installing a mural backsplash in your kitchen.

SAFETY

Proper preparation is the key to a successful tiling project. When you're excited about a new project, it's easy to overlook an important detail such as safety. You may be tempted to rush ahead without taking the time to properly prepare the work area or to acquaint yourself with the tools and materials you will be using. Overlooking any of these steps could create a safety hazard that can not only prevent you from successfully completing your job or damage the work you've already completed, but also lead to injury. Use good judgment and the resources available to you to prepare for a tiling project.

Make sure you understand the capabilities and limitations of your tools and materials. Before using a tiling tool, such as a wet saw, or handling a tiling material, such as thinset mortar, read the manufacturer's instructions completely, especially any warnings. Do not use tools that are not properly sharpened, and do not use power tools in a wet area. Make sure the work area is well lighted and ventilated.

The mortars, grouts, and sealants used for installing tile contain compounds that can irritate skin and lungs. Wear a good set of rubber gloves and a filter mask for protection. Invest in protective eyewear and wear it. Cutting, drilling, breaking, or removing tile can create sharp chips that can fly through the air. Put on work gloves to handle sharp or rough materials. Avoid carrying sharp objects in your pockets; use a tool belt designed to carry and protect your tools. Avoid loose clothing, pull back and secure long hair, and remove jewelry before working.

Keep a fully stocked first aid kit handy at your work site. Floor and wall tiling projects often call for you to spend a lot of time on your knees; a good set of knee pads with hard shells will protect your knees and allow you to work for a longer period of time.

PERMITS AND CODES

Depending on your city's building codes and the size of your residential remodeling project, you may be required to file for one or more building permits. To find your locality's building codes, call or visit the city's offices or check its website. The name of the department will vary. Generally you will need to complete an application for a permit and pay a fee. Inspections may be required while the job is in progress. Following codes may seem like a lot of extra work, but they are put into place to guard the health and safety of homeowners and anyone who comes into contact with an installation or project.

> **CHECK CODES WHEN PLANNING**
> While you're still in the planning stages of a project, such as tiling a fireplace surround, check local codes to ensure your project will be safe and in compliance with any local regulations.

Planning
YOUR TILING PROJECT

Tile is an ancient material long valued for its durability and nearly limitless decorative potential. Today new products and installation techniques have made this time-tested material more popular than ever. Tile is now well within the budget and talents of any serious do-it-yourselfer.

The options for color, texture, and shape are so varied that your biggest challenge may be choosing the best product and designs for your project. This chapter is intended to get your creative juices flowing by showcasing both practical and unique ways you can incorporate tile into your living space. Whether you want a traditional look, or a bold contemporary design, you'll find inspiration and ideas for every area of your home—kitchen, bath, living room, entryway, and outdoors.

You can also get ideas by visiting tile showrooms to select the colors and patterns that best suit your project. Once you've chosen the colors and patterns, select the type of tile right for the job (see pages 20–23). Compare prices by visiting your local home center or flooring retailer, or by browsing the Internet sites of tile manufacturers.

DRAMATIC IMPRESSIONS

Decorative tile can make a dramatic focal point that lends an impression of durability and quality to a room. A fireplace surround is an ideal place to showcase the full impact of decorative tiles.

MULTIFUNCTIONAL CERAMICS

Ceramic tile is noted for its water-resistant quality—one reason it is found in so many bathrooms. In bathrooms tile can be used on floors, walls, and countertops, and it is ideal for use in shower stalls and around bathtubs. With careful planning the entire room can be covered in an integrated design. If you live in a cool climate, bear in mind that tile flooring can be cold. Consider installing radiant heating in the setting bed (see page 18), an ideal way to keep your tile floor warm underfoot.

PROTECTIVE BEAUTY

Tile is a protective and decorative material to use around a fireplace or wood stove. See page 85 for precautions to take when installing tiles that will be subject to high temperatures.

INDOOR/OUTDOOR UNITY

One of the advantages of tile is that it can be used indoors and outdoors, beautifully merging areas of the home. You'll want to hire a professional to install the tile in a complex pool and patio area like this, but tiling a simple concrete patio or pool surround is well within the skill range of the average do-it-yourselfer.

UNEXPECTED DELIGHTS

If you love the look of tile, but don't have the budget to use it throughout your home, there are some small, unexpected areas where you can integrate the beauty of tile without spending a lot of money. For example a window sill is a small space that provides a unique focal point and easy installation. If you use decorative tile, you will want your curtains to be simple and not too elaborate, complementing the tile. Tiling furniture, such as an end table or coffee table, is another simple project. A coffee table can be updated by installing sealed heat-resistant natural stone tiles—you not only have the added beauty of natural stone, but built-in coasters as well! Also see "Building a Bathroom Mirror Tile Frame" on page 74.

TAKING TILE OUTDOORS

Using tile on your outdoor patio is ideal for both practical and aesthetic reasons. Take climate into consideration when using tile outdoors. In wet, freezing climates use vitreous or impervious tile marked freeze/thaw stable (see page 21). If you live in a warm, dry climate, you can use an unglazed tile. See page 89 for more details on taking tile outdoors.

'50s STYLE

This '50s inspired bathroom is beautifully executed with blue and yellow tiles that play off the color of the walls and cabinets. The listellos (border tiles) on the tub surround and wall break up the monotony of the blue tiles, and the dark mosaics used to border the floor add continued interest. See page 70 for more bathroom tiling ideas.

SURFACE VARIETY

This kitchen countertop incorporates a marble pastry slab into a ceramic tile surface. (See page 141 for how to set marble tile.) Grout lines, the area of a tile surface that is the most difficult to clean, are kept to a minimum with 6-inch tiles. Wood edging helps unify the countertop and the kitchen cabinetry.

STAGGERED CHECKERBOARD

These blue and white ceramic tiles set in a staggered checkerboard pattern are a practical surface for the kitchen backsplash, and become an integral component of the overall design, acting as a distinct focal point. A white grout was used as a design element—sealing grout after installation is imperative to maintaining its appearance. See page 149 for tips on keeping grout clean.

HEATED TILE FLOORS

Many homeowners shy away from installing tile in the bathroom or other living areas because they think the floor will be too cold. This does not have to be the case. Affordable electric floor heating comes in the form of an electric mat—similar to a heating pad—that is installed in the thinset mortar, and then controlled by a thermostat. As a do-it-yourselfer, you can install this type of electric floor heating yourself, but you may want to enlist the help of a professional to install the thermostat. Ask your tile supplier for a list of electric mat manufacturers and do-it-yourself tips.

COMBINING STYLE AND DURABILITY

Tile can be imaginatively put to work in all the hardworking areas of your house—almost anywhere you want to combine utility and beauty. Informal living areas, fireplaces, entryways, and, of course, kitchens and baths are all places where tile can enhance your home. In warm climates it has long been the material of choice for keeping floors and walls cool and dry. Though expensive initially the long life and low maintenance of tile usually negate the cost.

Desirable as tile is in many areas of the house, it might not be the perfect covering for every surface in your home. An overabundance of tile, especially in the same color and size, can be overwhelming and clinical-looking.

And in some situations tile's virtues can be a drawback: Tile is unforgiving when breakable objects fall on it. Tile floors can be cold when temperatures drop. Even the acoustic effect of tile should be kept in mind. Tile is great for singing in the shower but can create unpleasant echoes in large living areas.

> **STUNNING DETAIL**
> For an eye-catching focal point, use tile to cover and decorate a fireplace or to grace the surfaces around a wood stove. In otherwise bland rooms, ornamental tile work like this is all the architectural detail a room needs.

HARDWORKING UTILITY

Heavily trafficked informal living areas with access to the outdoors need a utilitarian but attractive surface. Tile makes a hardworking transition between indoors and outdoors and a pleasantly neutral setting for a variety of furnishing styles.

ENTRYWAY STYLE

Want protection from tracked in dirt and moisture without sacrificing style? An entryway is a place where you'll want to put your best foot forward with beautiful, low-maintenance tile. It will withstand lots of abuse but can be cleaned up quickly and thoroughly. Although small in terms of square footage, entryways make a strong style statement and are ideal places to invest in a tile installation. See page 44 for tiling an entryway.

SAFE AND CONVENIENT

In bathrooms tile protects underlying surfaces from water damage while offering additional safety and convenience, without compromising beauty. This bathroom adds distinction with decorative mirror and window tiles.
In bathrooms and other wet areas, be sure to choose tiles with a slip-resistant surface. Around tubs and showers, consider using smaller tiles, or even mosaics; the additional grout required by these tiles will make the floor less slippery. See page 70 for more bathroom tiling ideas.

When designing a tile installation, don't just think in terms of individual tiles. Instead think of the whole surface and of adjacent surfaces, textures, and colors. You can be decorative without having to rely heavily on decorative tiles.

If you want to use specially decorated tiles, be sure they are integrated with the overall scheme. Often you can buy decorative tiles to match the colors and sizes of the manufacturer's regular tiles. If you decide to use a few hand-painted tiles in a wall of commercially produced tiles, make sure the sizes and the colors of the tiles are compatible. If you plan to have a tile artist produce custom work for you, be sure to discuss the colors and function of your total project.

DECORATIVE DELIGHT
Decorative tiles integrated into a wall of field tiles create a stunning effect around this fireplace. Selective use of decorative tile, as shown here, makes a pleasing visual statement.

DESIGN DETAIL
Highlighting the backsplash above a cooktop with decorative tiles makes a striking statement in this kitchen. Limiting the use of decorative tiles to a small area such as this can increase their impact. Consider installing just a few decorative or colorful tiles within a field of standard tiles.

DURABLE FUN
Used to quirky good effect, this beautifully pieced-together tile job uses a mix of tiles to make colorful borders. This is a creative way to use the wide range of decorative tiles available, but be aware that if you mix tiles from different manufacturers, sizes and thicknesses can vary. You may find installation will be more complicated.

DESIGN WITHIN BUDGET

Because decorative and trim tiles can cost substantially more than regular field tiles, plan ahead to keep the finishing touches from destroying your budget. The secret is avoiding excessive use of the high-priced materials. For example, a few hand-painted or marble tiles mixed in among regular tiles will be more effective than scores of high-end tiles clamoring for attention. Although patterned border tiles look great around the perimeter of a room, you can achieve a similar effect using regular tiles in a different color. Limit the use of more expensive, decorative tiles and they will be more likely to attract attention.

USING TILE OUTSIDE

The moisture-resistance and decorative potential of tile makes it a popular material for use on patios and around swimming pools. Fountains, garden paths, and other walkways are also popular candidates for tiling projects. Until recently only homeowners in warm climates could consider outdoor tile: Materials and techniques simply were not available to protect tile from cracking under the stress of freeze/thaw conditions. Today, with newer materials and specialized installation procedures (see page 96), tile products can more easily withstand freezing temperatures. Every aspect of the installation must be planned to accommodate freezing conditions. Routine maintenance is critical as well; cracks in the grout or tile should be repaired immediately.

POOLSIDE SAFETY AND STYLE
Tile on a pool surround should be set on a concrete pad that is sloped away from the pool for drainage. Use slip-resistant tiles suitable for placement around exterior swimming pools. Installing tile on the inside of a swimming pool is best left to professional tile setters.

PERFECT FOR PATIOS
Stone tiles such as the ones on this enclosed patio are ideal for melding indoor and outdoor space. They look great, clean up quickly, and can withstand cold and wet weather. While hardy enough to handle outdoor weather and potted plants, they have a finished beauty that gives this space an almost indoor livability. Decorative ceramic tile on the fountain is an eye-catching feature of the enclosed patio.

CLIMATE CONTROL

Consider your climate when planning outdoor use of tiles. In an area where temperatures rarely dip below freezing, you can create an outdoor patio and path with ceramic tiles such as these. In colder climes opt for more rugged materials such as concrete or brick.

Good architectural design often goes unnoticed. A well-proportioned house or intelligently laid-out kitchen simply has a natural rightness about it. In the same way, a well-designed tile installation should look natural in its setting. When a surfacing material jumps out at you, the design has probably failed.

The age of your house, the decorating style you seek to capture, and your budget all affect the design you choose. Books, magazines, and tile brochures are the best sources of ideas. However be sure the types and patterns of tile you find attractive suit your space.

OBTAIN DESIGN ADVICE

Tile is a permanent surfacing material you'll be living with for a long time to come. It's well worth purchasing the advice of an architect or interior decorator if your tiling installation is part of a large remodeling job. But don't underestimate the expertise of flooring retailers and the tiling specialists at some home centers.

Come equipped with dimensions of the space you are tiling and magazine clippings of the styles and materials that you like. Retail specialists may be able to give you all the design guidance you need before launching your project.

PROPORTION TILE TO ROOM SIZE.

As a general rule tile size should be proportional to the size of the room. Small tiles generally work best in small rooms and large tiles look better in large rooms. Larger tiles seem less large when used on horizontal surfaces. Use larger tiles on lower surfaces; wall tiles or countertop tiles that are bigger than the floor tiles tend to make a room look top-heavy.

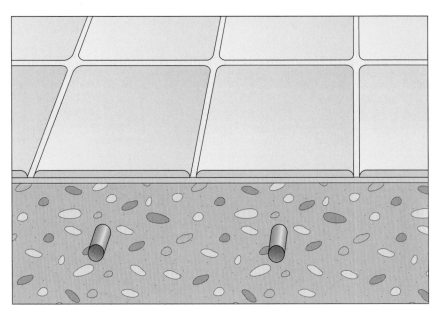

PLAN FOR COMFORT AS WELL AS STYLE.

Radiant heating systems, in which heated water passes through tubing embedded in or under the floor surface, are becoming increasingly popular. Tile is a great choice for the finish surface on a radiant floor. Because the tubing usually is embedded in concrete, the concrete pad can be used as an ideal setting bed for tile. Also tile is a highly conductive material that conveys heat quickly and efficiently. If you are tiling a new addition or need to improve heating in a room, consider incorporating a radiant heating system into the design.

DESIGNING WITH COLOR

With so many stunning tile colors readily available, it's tempting to wield a broad brush and let the color fly. But because today's fashionable color is often tomorrow's eyesore, white and almond tend to be the tones of choice for most homeowners. These light, neutral tones help brighten rooms and can coexist with other colors as your decorating schemes change. Many people think too much white or off-white is monotonous. Accent and border colors often cancel out this impression. In rooms with plenty of windows, consider using darker tiles to offset the ambient lighting.

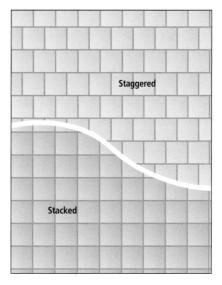

STAGGER OR STACK THE TILE.

Field tiles usually are installed in a stacked pattern or a staggered pattern. A stacked pattern is the easiest, and the clean, straight lines appeal to many people. Although they require careful alignment, staggered joints have a pleasingly retro look.

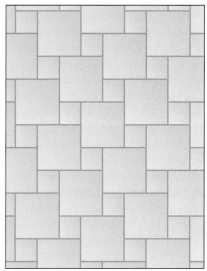

MAKE THE MOST OF ONE COLOR.

Using one color does not have to result in a plain-looking installation. Use tiles of different sizes to add a level of contrast. Consider different grout colors and grout joint sizes. Or use tiles with small variations in color.

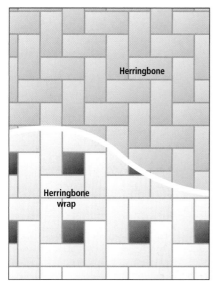

CONSIDER HERRINGBONE.

Plain rectangular tiles gain a new dimension when installed in a herringbone pattern. As a variation wrap a small square tile with rectangular tiles.

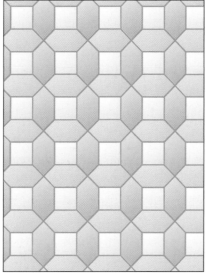

MIX SHAPES WITH COLORS.

Manufacturers offer tiles purposely sized to allow for mixing different shapes into a coherent whole. You can add further interest with this approach by using two or more colors as well.

DEFINE YOUR SPACE.

Borders help define the perimeters of a tile installation and can add a whole new level of interest to the surface. Here variously colored and sized tiles create a border surrounding a field of tiles installed diagonally.

Although simplicity is part of the universal appeal of ceramic tile (it is essentially a thin slab of baked clay), don't assume that just any tile will suit your project. Consider several factors as you select the right tile for the job: The material from which the tile is made (ceramic tile is made from clay; some tiles are actually slabs of stone milled into regular shapes), the degree of firing, the type of glaze, and the shape of the tile.

If you are planning several tiling projects for your home, you may want to contact one of the associations created by tile manufacturers, designers, retailers, and installation contractors. These groups have developed standards and acceptable practices relating to tile and tile installations.

The American National Standards Institute (ANSI) has prepared a list of minimal standards followed by all professionals in the industry. The Tile Council of America, Inc. (TCA) publishes the inexpensive annual *Handbook for Ceramic Tile Installation*, which incorporates the ANSI standards. Contact the TCA at Tile Council of America, Inc., 100 Clemson Research Blvd., Anderson, SC 29625, 864/646-8453, www.tileusa.com.

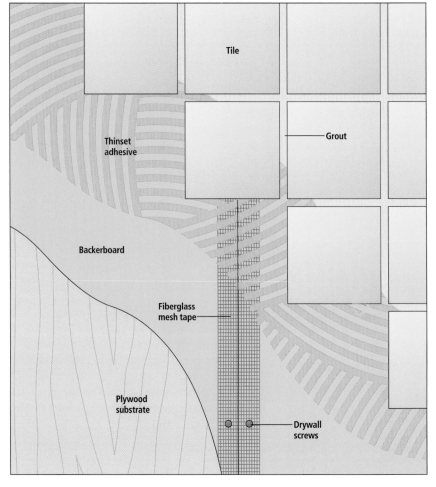

PLAN OUT A TYPICAL INSTALLATION.

Installing tile is a bit like making a sandwich: You proceed one layer at a time. The substrate, often plywood, is the layer in direct contact with the framing (studs for a wall installation or joists for a floor installation). Backerboard serves as the setting bed for the tiles themselves. Tiles form the outer layer. Adhesive is used to bond tile to the backerboard.

TILE INSTALLATION CHECKLIST

When you're planning a tile installation, check all of the boxes below that apply for the location of installation, special requirements, and the types of tile you are considering for the project. Review this information with the tile specialist or supplier to get the right tile for your specific application.

Location of Installation	Special Requirements	Type of Tile
☐ always dry or limited water exposure	☐ fire resistant	☐ glazed wall tile
☐ frequently wet	☐ stain resistant	☐ glazed floor tile
☐ interior	☐ crack resistant	☐ ceramic mosaic tile
☐ exterior	☐ color	☐ paver or quarry tile
☐ subject to freezing	☐ heavy use	☐ natural stone

WATER ABSORPTION

Clay absorbs water, and water can cause cracks in tiles and create damage beneath the surface. Ceramic tiles that have been kiln-dried longer and at higher temperatures absorb less water, but they also cost more. It makes sense to choose tiles rated precisely for the protection you need.

Tile Rating	Best Uses
Nonvitreous	This tile typically is used for decorative purposes only. It is intended for use indoors, in dry locations, such as a fireplace surround or a decorative frieze in a dining room.
Semivitreous	This type of tile is used indoors in dry to occasionally wet locations, such as a kitchen wall or behind a serving area in a dining room.
Vitreous	This multipurpose tile is used indoors and outdoors, in wet and dry locations for anything from bathroom floors and walls to a patio surface.
Impervious	Such tile generally is used only in hospitals, restaurants, and other commercial locations where thorough cleanliness is important.

CHOOSING DECORATIVE TILES

The term decorative tile is more descriptive than technical. It broadly defines tiles decorated by molding the clay, hand-painting a design, or affixing a decal to each tile before it is fired. Major tile manufacturers offer a multitude of tiles decorated with flowers, fruits, animals, and other images. Smaller specialty tile retailers may carry a wider selection of decorative tiles. Individual tile makers can be a particularly good source of original tiles. (Some will even make tiles to order.) Most decorative tiles serve as accents on walls, backsplashes, and fireplace surrounds.

▼ CAUTION

THE PERILS OF MIXING TILE

Have you ever run back and forth to the paint store trying to match the color of paint in a new can with the color already on your wall? If so you'll understand the difficulties of trying to match the colors, and sometimes even the exact sizes, of ceramic tiles. Avoid that frustration by buying more tile than you think you will need. Save some of the leftovers for future repairs, and return unopened boxes for a refund.

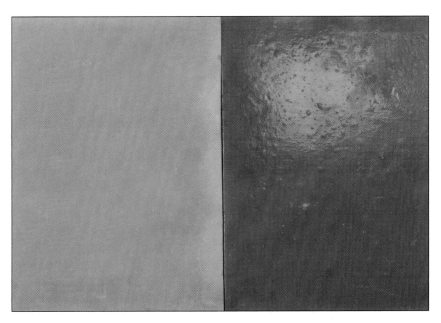

CHOOSE A GLAZE.

A glaze is a protective and decorative coating, often colored, fired onto the surface of tiles. Glazes can be glossy, matte, or textured. Glazing is not related directly to the water absorption categories shown above. Although glazing does keep moisture from penetrating the top surface, the unglazed sides and bottoms of the tile don't have the same protection.

Selecting the right tile for the job *(continued)*

SELECT THE TYPE OF CERAMIC TILE.

Modern ceramic tile is made from refined clay, usually mixed with additives and water, then hardened in a kiln. Several different types of tile are created using that process. Quarry tiles are unglazed and vitreous tiles, usually ½-inch thick and used for flooring. Pavers are ⅜-inch-thick vitreous floor tiles and are available glazed or unglazed.

CHOOSE DIFFERENT SIZES AND SHAPES.

Square tiles are the most common and the easiest to install. But rectangles, hexagons, and other shapes are readily available. An easy and inexpensive way to add interest to a tile installation is to mix shapes, sizes, and colors; tile retailers and home centers offer a wide range of options.

CONSIDER STONE TILE.

Use natural stone tile on floors, walls, and countertops. Marble (see above left), granite, flagstone, and slate (see above right) are widely available; other types of stone may be available in your area. Dimensioned (also called gauged) stone is cut to a uniform size and thickness and can be installed much like ceramic tile. Hand-split, sometimes called cleft stone tiles vary in size and thickness.

OTHER TILING CHOICES

Cement-bodied tiles are made with a concrete mix that is extruded or cast, then cured to form a strong, dense tile. They usually are stained to look like pavers, quarry tile, stone, or brick. Often you can buy them with a factory-applied sealer. Brick-veneer tile is made like ceramic tile, but with a coarser body that simulates brick. Terrazzo is manufactured with small pieces of granite or marble set in mortar, then polished. Precast terrazzo tiles are available for floors and walls.

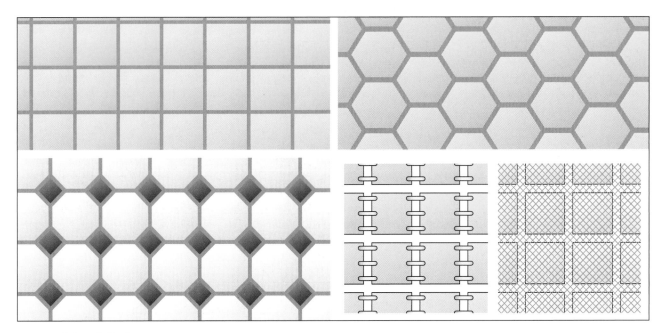

USE MOSAIC TILE.

Mosaic tiles are 1- or 2-inch squares or similarly sized hexagons or octagons mounted together as a larger unit. Most commercially available mosaics are vitreous and freeze/thaw stable and can be used on most tiling projects. Mosaic tiles are sold almost exclusively mounted on sheets or joined with adhesive strips. Back-mounted mosaic tiles are much easier to install than individual tiles. They can be mounted with standard thinset adhesive and grout.

NOMINAL VS. ACTUAL SIZE

Most do-it-yourselfers learn quickly that when buying lumber, a 2×4 doesn't measure 2 inches by 4 inches. The tile trade has a similar discrepancy. Individual ceramic tiles are often sold with dimensional names that describe their installed size, that is, the size of the tile plus a standard grout joint. Thus 6×6-inch tiles measure $\frac{1}{8}$ inch shorter in each direction. The actual size will be $5\frac{7}{8} \times 5\frac{7}{8}$ inches. Only when installed with a $\frac{1}{8}$-inch grout joint will the installed size of the tile be about 6×6 inches. Always check the actual size of the tiles before you buy them.

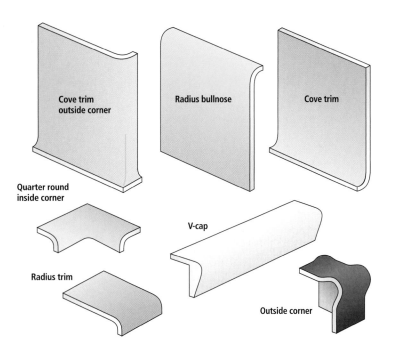

Cove trim outside corner

Radius bullnose

Cove trim

Quarter round inside corner

Radius trim

V-cap

Outside corner

DETERMINE THE RIGHT TRIM TILES.

In general tiles are divided into field tiles, which are flat, and trim tiles, shaped irregularly to turn corners or define the edges of an installation. There are dozens of trim-tile profiles, and the names of each can be confusing. When choosing tiles be sure to check the availability of these specialty tiles and select a style with trim tiles suitable for your project.

Tile has been a popular flooring choice for years, and recent techniques in glazing and sealing allow for a wider range of tiles to be appropriate for the wear and tear that floors receive. Although more choices give the consumer more options, they also add to the confusion of choosing the right tile for the right space. To avoid becoming overwhelmed, stick with the basics and ask yourself the following questions: What type of material is best suited for this space? Does the material need a finish? What color will complement the space and its surrounding areas? What size and shape is appropriate for the size of the space? Do I want to add any decorative touches, such as decorative tiles or patterns?

As a do-it-yourselfer, it is wise to double-check with your supplier to be sure that the tiles you choose are appropriate for the space and the amount of wear and tear they will receive. Also check out the Floor Tile table on page 26 for a brief overview of your floor tile options.

Glazed ceramic for floors
A glazed ceramic is a clay tile treated with liquid glass and hardened by firing under extreme temperatures. It is a water-resistant tile found in almost any color or texture imaginable. The hardness of the tile depends on the temperature of the fire and the length of time the tile was fired. When choosing a glazed ceramic tile for floors, make sure the glaze is hard enough to handle the foot traffic it will endure. Use a wet saw for cutting and latex-reinforced thinset mortar for installation.

Quarry
Quarry tiles are a natural-looking, durable tile made from red clay by extrusion. They are usually vitreous (see page 21) and great for outdoor use. No two tiles are alike and their thicknesses vary. They are typically unsealed and good for patios and sidewalks because they are naturally slip-resistant when wet. However, because they are unglazed, they are susceptible to stains, so you will want to use a sealer to protect the tile. They come in a variety of sizes ranging from 6×6 to 12×12 inches. Use a wet saw for cutting and a latex-reinforced thinset mortar for installation.

Cement-bodied tiles
Cement-bodied tiles are a durable and inexpensive tile made of sand-mix concrete. They are not as natural

> **TILE ART**
> This hallway's terra-cotta pavers are playfully enhanced by colorful shards of blue and red tile, turning the design of the floor into an actual work of art. This design creates a fun and joyful attitude that draws you into the living space.

looking as stone but come in various shapes and colors. They are great for all flooring surfaces but may not hold up when installed outdoors in a freezing climate (check with your supplier). They stain easily so use a sealer. Use a wet saw for cutting and latex-reinforced thinset mortar for installation.

Porcelain

Porcelain tiles are a durable tile that can stand in for several different materials, such as marble and granite, but are waterproof and more stain-resistant. Porcelain is ideal for both interior and exterior floors and comes in a side variety of colors and textures. If you're not an expert, you might not be able to tell the difference between porcelain and marble. Use a wet saw for cutting and a latex-reinforced thinset mortar for installation.

VARIED SIZES
Different sizes of the same slate tiles are used throughout the kitchen on the floor and backsplash. Larger tiles are used on the floor, and the backsplash tiles are staggered to follow the lines of the oven hood. Listellos on the backsplash break up the monotony of the slate.

DUAL DESIGN
Black and white porcelain tiles create a dramatic but functional look for this combination dining and work space. The tiles are placed at a diagonal to create visual interest. A rug softens the hard lines of the tile and helps create a natural divider between the two spaces.

Planning your floor tiling project *(continued)*

Natural stone

Natural stone tiles include tile such as marble, granite, limestone, and slate. Stone tiles stain easily, so make sure they are well sealed. Because not all stone tiles are durable enough for flooring, consult with your supplier to ask if the tile is appropriate for the space you're tiling. Also, because no two stones are alike, buy additional tiles in case the ones you are setting do not match up well enough.

Terra-cotta

Terra-cotta tiles come from all over the world, including Mexico, France, and Italy. Terra-cotta is available in a variety of earth-tone colors—often the tile will have a look distinctive to its country of origin. Terra-cotta should not be used outdoors if you live in a freezing climate, but it is great for all other flooring opportunities. Use a wet saw for cutting and a latex-reinforced thinset mortar for installation.

Mosaic

Mosaic tiles are considered mosaic due to their size and shape. They generally range from $1/2 \times 1/2$ to 2×2 inches square and can be made of ceramic, glass, or natural stone. They are usually available in "sheets" ranging from 12×12 to 12×24 inches square, making installation simpler. During installation use a knife to cut the mosaic sheets. If your mosaics are translucent, be sure to use a white mortar so the clarity of the color is not compromised.

MOSAIC DESIGN

This one-of-a-kind mosaic tile floor took great planning and forethought. There's no mistaking the country feel of the kitchen. When planning such an intricate design, you want to plan ahead and use graph paper to make a scale drawing. See page 138 for tips on working with mosaic tiles.

FLOOR TILE				
Type	**Description**	**Standard size**	**Benefits**	**Drawbacks**
Glazed ceramic	A clay tile treated with a liquid glass, then hardened by baking under extreme temperatures.	8×8 or 12×12	Durability.	Smooth finishes can be slippery when wet; select an appropriate finish.
Quarry	Made from red clay, by extrusion. Sturdy, mostly unglazed.	6×6 8×8 12×12	Vitreous—ideal for outdoor use.	Stain easily if untreated.
Porcelain	White clay baked at extreme temperatures, resulting in a durable tile.	12×12	Waterproof and stain-resistant.	More expensive
Terra-cotta	Unglazed tiles in earth tones.	Sizes and shapes vary—squares, rectangles, hexagons, and more.	A variety of sizes and shapes that look great with decorative ceramics.	Need to be sealed.
Natural stone	Includes marble, granite, slate, onyx, travertine, quartzite, and limestone.	Sizes range from 12×12 to 24×24.	Repel moisture (not slate or some marble).	Natural, so no two tiles are exactly alike; higher cost.
Cement-bodied	Durable. Made of sand-mix concrete.	Sizes range from 2×2 to 12×12.	Can be stained in any color; inexpensive.	Stain easily.

Decorative

Decorative tiles can turn your tiling project into a work of art. You can truly customize your space, making it unique to your taste and style. Decorative tiles come in various shapes, sizes, colors, and designs. The key is to use them appropriately throughout the design. Draw your pattern ahead of time on graph paper to save time during the actual installation.

Baseboard

Baseboards play a crucial role in the final appearance of your newly tiled floor. The easiest way to trim the floor is to reinstall the baseboards that were previously on the wall. For a more integrated look you can install baseboards using bullnose tiles of the same tile used on the floor. Or you can get creative and use a natural stone of a different color for a more dramatic look. Stone, however, usually does not have the radius edge that is typical of baseboards.

SEALING TILES AND GROUT

It depends on the type of tile you're working with whether you will seal the tile or just the tile grout. If you're working with a glazed ceramic tile, you need to seal only the grout joints. Sealing the grout joints in bathrooms and kitchens is highly recommended, because it will protect against mildew and other water damage. It's best to wait a couple weeks before applying the sealant, so the grout has plenty of time to set. If you are working with a porous, nonvitreous material that easily absorbs water and stains, you will want to seal the tiles before installation. To maintain the tiles, reapply a sealer about once a year.

REINFORCING THE FLOOR

If installed correctly tile can last for decades. Before installing the tile, it's important to check the strength of the floor. Wood floors naturally have some give, but you want to make sure they will be able to provide a solid base to prevent tiles from cracking. To check the strength of the floor, start by jumping up and down on it. If you feel any movement, take steps to reinforce the floor.

A popular method for strengthening a floor is called "sistering." This technique involves attaching another piece of wood alongside the joists. First measure the current joists and have new joists cut to fit. Then apply construction adhesive and attach the new joist. You can use clamps to hold the joists in place while they set. Finally drive screws or nails to hold the sister joist in place. Continue until all joists are secure.

If you will be working on the second story of your home, you may want to enlist the help of a professional.

SMOOTH TRANSITIONS
The gray stone tiles used in this kitchen enhance the stainless-steel cooktop. They also make a smooth transition into the dining area, incorporated into an interesting block design mixed with neutral stone. See page 36 for instructions on tiling floors.

Because wall tiles are applied to a vertical surface, they are manufactured to be thinner and lighter than floor tiles. Although you want floor tile to be durable and slip-resistant, you want wall tile, if used in a kitchen or bath, to be waterproof and stain-resistant. Wall tiles don't suffer the wear and tear that floor tiles do; let the style of the tile be the driving force in selection. Wall tiles typically are less expensive than floor tiles and come in a wider range of colors. Most suppliers have wall tiles that will complement your floor tiles. One of the keys to successfully planning your wall tile project is to decide where you want the focal point to be, keeping in mind what color, size, and shape will complement the space and, of course, what your budget can stand. See pages 66–69 for more on tiling backsplashes.

Glazed ceramic for walls

Glazed ceramic tile is made of clay that has been treated with liquid glass, then hardened by firing under extreme temperatures. Glazed ceramics are ideal for walls because they are impervious to moisture. There are thousands of colors, types, shapes, and textures from which to choose. For installation use a snap cutter or nibbling tool. Use a latex-reinforced thinset mortar, and use caulk when a joint butts up against another material.

Glass

Like glazed ceramic tiles, glass tiles are perfect for kitchens and baths because they are impervious to water. See "Tiling with Mosaic Glass Tile" on page 68. Glass tiles allow for a lot of creative expression as well; however, you must be a bit more careful in installation. If the glass tile is translucent, use a white thinset mortar because the gray thinset mortar may show through and affect the clarity of the color.

Metal

Metal tiles can provide a polished and elegant look to your walls and backsplashes. They are available in brass, copper, stainless steel, and even zinc. Metal tiles are typically the standard thickness of ceramic tiles, allowing you to easily integrate them into your design. You can use soap and water to clean, and olive oil to remove fingerprints. They are expensive and you will need a wet saw to cut them.

STAGGERED BEAUTY
This bathroom's wall tiles are staggered, providing a retro look. The blue tiles offset the black-and-white mosaic floor nicely, while the stainless-steel mirror complements the tile and adds depth to the small space. See page 76 for more on tiling showers and tubs.

Mosaic

Mosaic wall tiles can allow for maximum creative expression as they are available in a variety of colors, shapes, and types of tile. Mosaics are any tiles 2×2 inches square or less, and they usually come in 12×12 sheets. Because mosaics are small and easy to handle, they are ideal for tiling a rounded or curved surface. During installation use a knife to cut the mosaic sheets, then set them in organic mastic. Take special care to set them firmly in the mastic.

Trim

After you install field tiles on a wall, you must complete the look with a trim tile to finish off the rough edges. Trim tiles give your wall a complete, polished look. The most common wall trim is the bullnose tile. The surface bullnose tile has one rounded edge, as does the radius bullnose, but the radius bullnose has a deeper curve and is usually used for countertops. There are several other trim tiles used for corners and countertop edging. It is best to buy your trim tile from the same supplier as your field tile, to ensure a cohesive look.

OLD-WORLD CHARM
The black, staggered tiles add distinction to the old-world charm of this bathroom. The light-colored grout adds needed contrast, while the window provides natural light so the space does not appear too dark. See page 70 for more bathroom tiling ideas.

ARE THE WALLS STIFF ENOUGH?

Before you begin your wall tiling project make sure you will work with a flat surface that is rigid enough to hold the tile without flexing, which will create cracks. Press your hand against a panel between two wall studs. If the surface flexes, you need to strengthen the wall. See page 52 for details on wall substrates.

Planning your wall tiling project *(continued)*

Listello or border

Listellos are commonly referred to as border tiles. They are more ornate than trim tiles and are usually installed as accent pieces to draw the eye to a focal point or to seamlessly transition from one material to the next. A border tile is usually the same width as a field tile but its height can vary. They may be used as a trim tile in certain situations. Because of their decorative quality they tend to be more expensive.

> **FINISHED EDGES**
> Listello tiles can be used as trim tiles to cover exposed edges, add an accent to an otherwise plain layout, or create a transition from one space to the next. They are decorative and will give any tiling project a finished, professional look. The art tiles seen in the background can add visual interest to walls and backsplashes.

RENEWED INTEREST
You can renew your fireplace surround to anchor and establish the theme of your room. This fireplace surround of blue and white decorative tiles creates an undeniable focal point, without detracting from the other decor in the room. See page 84 for tips on renewing a fireplace surround.

See page 84 for tips on renewing a fireplace surround.

ACCOUNT FOR TILE BREAKAGE

If you are using more than one kind of tile, make sure they are the same size and thickness. It's wise to use tiles from the same supplier. Always purchase an extra 10 percent of tiles to account for tile breakage.

PUT YOUR PLAN ON PAPER

When planning a tile project, it is always a good idea to draw your design on graph paper before starting, especially if you want to use more than one color or create a pattern.

EYE-CATCHING BACKSPLASH
The alternating red and white glazed ceramic tiles used on this kitchen's backsplash are both practical and eye-catching. They complement the red and white stripes on the far wall and the black and white diagonally-set floor tiles. See pages 66–67 for step-by-step instructions for tiling a backsplash.

SELECTING WALL TILE

Type	Description	Standard size	Benefits	Drawbacks
Glazed ceramic	A nonvitreous tile with a glaze. Not as strong as a glazed ceramic floor tile.	3"×3" 4"×4" 6"×6"	Self-spacing; wide variety of choices.	So many choices can make it difficult to decide what's right for your space.
Glass	Glass tiles are often eco-friendly, coming from recycled goods. Their colors can be swirled, metallic, or even iridescent.	¾" × ¾" mosaics up to 12"×12" tiles.	Impervious to stains and moisture.	Special care in installation.
Metal	Usually used as accent tiles, made of stainless steel, copper, brass, and zinc.	4"×4" and 6"×6"	Create a dramatic statement.	Expensive.
Mosaic	Small tiles. Shapes vary from squares to hexagons and octagons.	¾"×¾" up to 2"×2". Sheets are typically 12"×12" or 12"×24" inches.	Due to their size, perfect for working in small or rounded spaces.	Special care in installation.
Trim	Tiles used to cover exposed edges.	Typically the same size as the field tiles used.	Provide the final touch to give the wall a professional look.	Higher cost than field tiles.
Listello or border	Decorative tiles used to provide a finished look—sometimes used as a trim tile.	¼" to 4".	Available in a variety of shapes, colors, and sizes.	Higher cost per tile.

Tile
PROJECTS

Integrating tile into the design of your home can add both form and function—combining rich textures and color with time-tested durability and practicality. If installed correctly, tiles can withstand wear and tear indoors, and hold up to the elements outdoors far longer than any other flooring, wall, or countertop application. With patience and fortitude, you can have the satisfaction of designing and executing many tiling projects on your own.

Before beginning a project be methodical; take time to step back and observe the space you want to transform. Ask yourself—what is my vision for the space? How does it complement the rest of my home? Does my budget allow for the materials I need?

The previous chapter explored how to choose the right tile for your project and the details that go into planning a project. This chapter's projects are designed to spark your creativity as you exercise your tiling skills and execute your plan. Learn to tile your kitchen and bath, from floors to walls to countertops. Consider adding a pattern to your entryway or a mural to your kitchen backsplash. Give your fireplace a facelift or plan a wood stove surround. Take your tile projects outside—jazz up your outdoor grill with a tile countertop, or even tile a bistro table for your patio with leftover broken tiles. "Tile Projects" will guide you step-by-step, but don't be afraid to generate your own design ideas.

WARMTH AND PRACTICALITY

The richness of this kitchen's style is created by the placement of the natural stone tiles on the countertops and backsplash, producing a warm, inviting, seamless look. The terra-cotta pavers set diagonally add practicality and flair to the floor design. See page 58 for more countertop tiling ideas.

A FOCAL POINT

This fireplace surround creates a strong focal point and updates the living space. A border of mosaics sets off the dramatic black and white glazed ceramic tiles. See page 84 for renewing a fireplace surround.

PLAYFUL STYLE

This playful kitchen incorporates beautiful glazed ceramic countertops and brightly colored shards of tile that swirl through the kitchen—accenting the terra-cotta pavers and leading to a beautiful outdoor space. See page 40 for step-by-step instructions on tiling a kitchen floor.

DESIGNING A TILE FLOOR

Floor tiles are available in so many sizes, shapes, and colors that the most difficult part of the project often is deciding on a pattern. Not only do you have many choices in tile color and texture, but you can achieve different effects by adjusting the tiles and grout joints. Use one color of tile with matching grout to achieve a unified look, often welcomed in small rooms. Or use a contrasting grout to call attention to the individual tiles. Alternate two or more colors of tiles in a pattern or randomly to enliven a room. If you opt for this approach, look for a neutral grout that blends well with your tile colors. Keep the scale of the room and the tile design in harmony: In small spaces use patterns on a small scale and limit color variety. In larger rooms feel free to experiment with bolder contrasts.

HANDSOME UNITY
Often it's best to let the material set the tone. In this bathroom luxurious marble tiles form a handsome setting for a rug that imitates mosaic tile. Running the tile up the tub surround and wall gives a clean unity to the room. Accent colors can change over the years with this design choice; a beautiful groundwork is in place.

GRACEFUL PATTERNS
The graceful sweep of this tiled entryway perfectly suits the contemporary style of this home, while providing hardworking utility where it is needed. The pattern of the tiles is straightforward; it's the shape of the platform that sets this floor apart. If your project calls for revising your floor structure, plan ahead to take the final configuration of the tiled surface into consideration. Often it is best after purchasing tile to do a dry run to determine the best possible pattern, and then frame the floor.

SUITABLE CONTRASTS

The unusual offset of this herringbone pattern suits the shape of the space and is suitable for a variety of decorating styles. Set at a slight angle to the outermost bay, there is an informality to the layout that contrasts pleasantly with the formality of the furnishings.

CLASSIC FLEXIBILITY

A bathroom classic, sheet-laid hexagonal tiles in basic black and white will serve for decades as a backdrop for whatever accent colors used in the room. Another benefit of this tile design is its structural flexibility. Should the substrate deteriorate over the years, cracks will tend to follow the grout lines rather than run through the tiles themselves.

TILING FLOORS

Unless your home was seriously underbuilt, your floors are strong enough so you can install carpeting or another type of resilient flooring with confidence. But ceramic tile has more demanding requirements. The weight of the tiles is not usually the problem; deflection is. If a ceramic tile floor flexes, grout and even tiles can crack. If you have any doubts about the strength of the floor, ask a contractor to inspect it before you begin tiling.

Sometimes a bouncy floor can be firmed up by driving screws through the subflooring and into joists. Or you may have to add another subfloor layer, or even beef up the joists. However, if you build up the floor so much that the new tile surface will be ½ inch or more higher than an adjacent floor surface, it will look and feel awkward. That's why in some situations it is simply not practical to lay a ceramic tile floor.

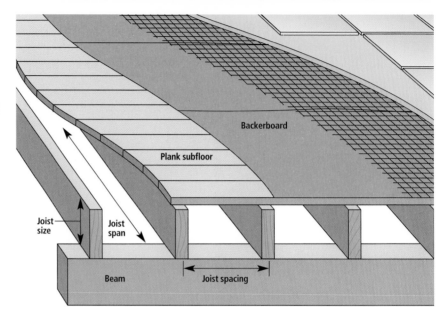

ANATOMY OF A FLOOR.

Floor strength is determined by the size of the joists, the length of the joists' span between supports, and the amount of space between joists. If your joists have spacing larger than 16 inches, for instance, then you will need an extra strong subfloor. If you are not sure whether your floor is strong enough, consult with a professional. Plywood is the best subfloor material, but many older homes have strong subfloors made of 1× lumber.

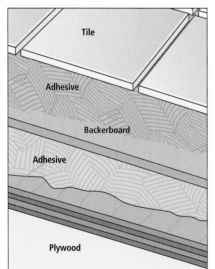

BACKERBOARD.

Older installations set tiles on a thick bed of mortar. Backerboard is an excellent modern-day substitute. Use as thick a board as possible, installed over a plywood subfloor. See pages 130–131 for cutting and installation instructions.

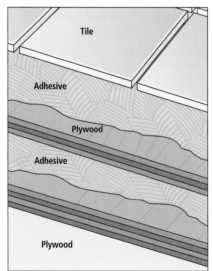

PLYWOOD.

Although plywood is somewhat soft and flexible, it also has great strength. When two sheets are laminated together, the result is a very firm surface. Use plywood as a subsurface in dry areas only.

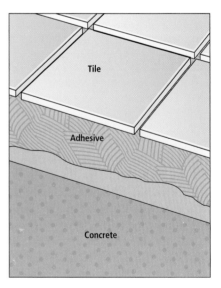

CONCRETE.

Concrete makes the best subsurface and works well for straightening out-of-level floors. Do not use curing or acceleration chemicals if you pour a concrete floor; they may interfere with the thinset bond. An older concrete surface must be sound; tiling will not strengthen it.

PREPARING A WOOD FLOOR.

When tiling directly over plywood, it is best to install two layers of ⅝-inch-minimum plywood, rather than one thick sheet. Use exterior-grade plywood for the top layer. The edges should always fall over a joist, but stagger the sheets so the joints do not fall directly over each other. Coat the bottom sheet with construction adhesive before setting the top sheet in place. Leave a gap of ⅛ inch or more around all edges of the top sheets, including at the joints. Fasten the plywood with screws or ringshank nails. If an existing plywood subfloor is strong enough, sand the surface thoroughly, then vacuum. Talk to your tile dealer about the best adhesive to use.

If the existing floor is composed of 1× or 2× planking in good condition, drive screws into joists wherever it seems loose, and perhaps install a layer of plywood over it. If it has cracks and does not feel strong, remove the planking and install plywood.

PREPARING A CONCRETE FLOOR FOR TILE.

Concrete is a great base for tile, as long as it is structurally sound and flat. Some slabs may actually be too smooth, and should be scruffed up a bit by grinding with an abrasive wheel. Do not install tile over concrete that was treated with a curing or acceleration chemical when it was poured. These additives will prevent thinset or adhesive from bonding properly.

If you are uncertain about whether or not such additives were used, try to locate the builder of the house or concrete contractor. They may have a record of the job. You can also test the slab yourself by sprinkling water on it. If the water isn't absorbed, the concrete was probably treated. Apply a bonding agent to the surface or add a subfloor.

INSTALL PLYWOOD.

For the top layer of plywood, leave ⅛-inch gaps between the sheets to allow for expansion. Fasten with screws or ringshank nails in a 6-inch grid in the field, and every 4 inches at the joints and around the perimeter.

BEEF UP A WOOD FLOOR.

Strengthen a weak subfloor by installing wood or metal cross bridging between joists. Close small gaps between joists and the existing subfloor with shims.

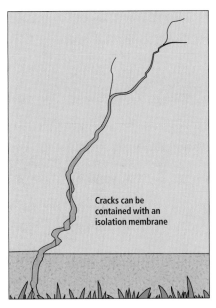

Cracks can be contained with an isolation membrane

DEALING WITH CRACKS.

Cover small cracks in concrete with an isolation membrane (see page 118). Cracks that result in uneven surfaces indicate underlying structural problems; do not tile over such a surface.

Patch uneven surfaces

FILL IN LOW SPOTS.

Clean out low spots in a concrete slab and fill with thinset mortar. Use a trowel or straightedge to level the surface.

Tiling floors *(continued)*

REPLACING BASEBOARDS

As long as you're tiling your floor, you may want to update your baseboards as well. New tile may emphasize your old baseboard's imperfections.

Old vinyl cove base can get pretty ratty-looking. Install new cove base after the tile job is done. Make sure that the new material is as wide as the original, or you will have an ugly line on the wall. Attach with cove base adhesive.

The base shoe gets banged up, in time too. So go ahead and replace it. Use stain or paint on it, then cut it with a miter box and fasten it with finishing nails.

REMOVE THE BASEBOARD.

Before tiling a floor, remove the baseboard from the surrounding walls. If the joint between the baseboard and wall is sealed with paint, score it with a utility knife first. Pull the vinyl cove base away from the wall with a putty knife. If it resists removal, try heating the vinyl with a hair dryer to loosen the adhesive. Use a pry bar to remove wooden baseboard. Protect the wall with a thin piece of wood. If your baseboard has a shoe— a small rounded molding at the bottom—just remove that.

TRIM CASING AND DOORS.

It is usually not a good idea to remove door casings. But cutting tile to fit around casing is difficult and usually leads to a sloppy-looking job. Trim the bottom of the casing, and fit the tiles beneath it.

With the subfloor installed, place a tile up against the casing. Lay a handsaw on the tile as you cut through the casing.

Place tiles on the floor near a door to make sure it will swing freely after the tiles are installed. If not use the tiles and a pencil to scribe a cut line at the bottom of the door. Allow for a gap of at least ¼ inch. Remove the door by popping out the hinge pins. Place masking tape along the bottom of the most visible side of the door, and mark a cut line. Cut through the tape using a circular saw with a clamped straightedge as a guide.

CHECK FLOORS FOR LEVEL.

Use a carpenter's level and a straight board to check the floor for level and to find any spots that are not flat. If the entire floor is out of level with the wall, it can still be tiled. If you plan to extend tile up the wall, however, you should consider leveling the floor or using tapered baseboard to make the transition attractive.

PLANNING TRANSITIONS

A newly tiled floor may be higher than the adjoining floor. Plan your approach to these transitions before you begin any work. The most common technique is to install a transitional piece called a threshold. You can buy metal or wood thresholds that are sloped to ease the transition. Some are designed to be installed after the tile is laid and grouted; others should be installed at the same time as you lay the tile. Using a tablesaw, you can make your own threshold out of oak or another hardwood.

LEVEL A FLOOR.

Small bumps in the floor must be dealt with before you begin tiling. If the wood subfloor comes up in places, try driving screws through the flooring and into a joist to level it out. You may be able to take out small high spots with a belt sander.

To straighten out dips and low areas, or to level an entire floor, use a self-leveling floor patch compound. These are made by manufacturers of tile adhesive.

Place barriers where necessary to keep the compound where it belongs. Mix the dry ingredients with water, then pour it on the floor. The mixture will level itself out to a certain degree, but use a long, flat trowel to help things along. The compound should be cured and ready for tiling within a few hours. Most self-leveling compounds are intended to function at depths no greater than 1 inch. If the work seems intimidating, talk to a contractor about preparing a level subfloor for you.

TILING A KITCHEN FLOOR

Tiling a kitchen floor can be a major disruption to any household. This project affects access to food, meal preparation, and traffic patterns through the kitchen. Some preparation can be done well in advance of the tiling; some cabinets can be removed, new subflooring applied, and doors removed. For the tiling itself, set aside a long weekend so the kitchen can be back in operation as quickly as possible.

YOU'LL NEED

TIME: 3–4 days to prepare, lay out, and tile an average-size kitchen.

SKILLS: Disconnecting and removing appliances, removing base cabinets, preparing a subfloor, tiling and grouting the floor.

TOOLS: Screwdriver, hammer, pry bar, putty knife, tiling tools.

KNEE PADS

Tiling floors is hard on your knees. In addition to the stress of kneeling much of the time, your knees are vulnerable to injury from tools and pieces of material left around the work area. That's why contractors who spend a lot of time working at floor level consider knee pads essential. For occasional use on wood or tile floors, nonmarring foam, rubber, or rubber-capped pads are a good choice. For heavy-duty protection, but less comfort, buy skateboarder-type knee pads that have a hard nylon shield on the front.

1 ASSESS THE CABINETS.

As a general rule, there is no need to install tile where it will be covered by cabinet bases or other permanent fixtures. Instead use a thin pry bar and stiff putty knife to remove the toe-kick and any molding along the floor. Set tile up to the cabinet. After all the tile is installed and grouted, trim the upper edge of the toe-kick to fit and reinstall it and the molding.

2 REMOVE CABINETS WHERE NEEDED.

Sometimes cabinets must be removed to take out the old flooring or to replace the subfloor. Remove fasteners holding the countertop in place, and the screws that join cabinets to each other and to the wall. In addition remove overlapping pieces of toe-kick and other molding.

CONSIDER THE APPLIANCES.

One of the issues you will have to address is whether or not to tile beneath appliances. Freestanding appliances, such as refrigerators, ranges, and dishwashers, should be removed from the kitchen to install tile underneath the appliance location. It is also best to tile beneath built-in appliances, although the work can be trickier. By tiling beneath a built-in dishwasher, for example, you raise the floor level so the dishwasher will no longer fit under the countertop. You can raise the countertop a bit to accommodate the appliance. Adjustments may also have to be made in the plumbing connections. Despite these problems, think of how your kitchen floor would look if it was empty. Untiled spaces where appliances usually sit would be unattractive to potential home buyers.

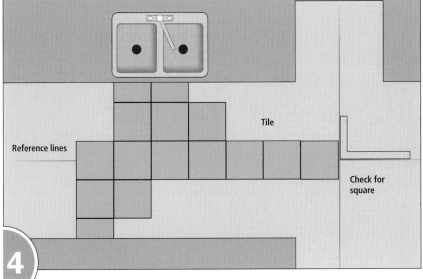

LAY OUT THE JOB.

At the center of the floor, mark perpendicular reference lines with a pencil or chalk line. (In odd-shape rooms you may want to center the layout on the most visible section of the floor rather than in the center of the room.) Check to make sure that the lines are square (see pages 123–125). Using appropriate spacers, if needed with your tile, dry-set tiles along the reference lines to check the layout. Adjust the layout to minimize the number of cut tiles and to avoid creating any extremely small pieces.

SET THE TILES.

Begin at the intersecting reference lines and spread thinset mortar over a small area. Do not cover the lines. Set properly spaced tiles. Use a beater block (see page 112) after setting each section of tiles. Check alignment as you go.

TILING BATHROOM FLOORS

Tile is a great material for bathroom floors: tough, attractive, and easy to clean. Many bathrooms have tile on every surface; plan ahead if you want to resurface your walls, countertops, or tub and shower areas. One of the great joys of tiling a bathroom is the chance to experiment with bold colors and unusual designs.

A typical bathroom floor does not require a waterproof installation, although you should choose tiles and setting materials suitable for a surface that will get wet from time to time.

YOU'LL NEED

TIME: 2–3 days for an average bathroom floor.

SKILLS: Removing and resetting a toilet, preparing a subfloor, laying out and tiling a floor.

TOOLS: Wrench, hacksaw, tiling and grouting tools.

REMOVING SINKS

If you have a pedestal or wall-mounted sink with legs, remove it before you start to tile. Shut off the water supply and disconnect the supply lines. Remove the trap with a pipe wrench. Unbolt and remove the top of a pedestal sink, then unbolt and remove the pedestal. (One-piece pedestal sinks are bolted to the floor and wall.) Remove the legs of a wall-mounted sink and pull the sink up and off of the mounting bracket. You may also want to remove a vanity, depending on its position.

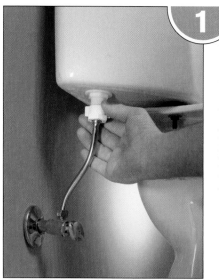

1 REMOVE THE TOILET.

When tiling a bathroom floor, it is easier in the long run to remove the toilet and tile up to the closet flange. The tile will look better and pose fewer maintenance problems. Shut off the water supply and disconnect the supply line. Flush the toilet, then sponge the remaining water from the tank. Unbolt and remove the tank.

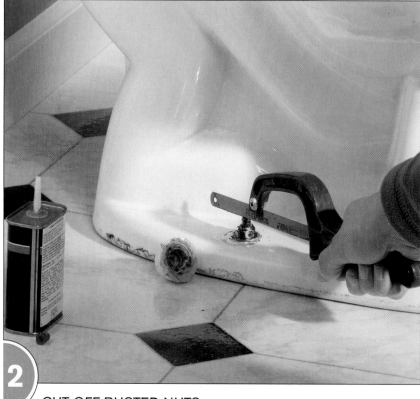

2 CUT OFF RUSTED NUTS.

Pry off the decorative caps, then unscrew the flange nuts. If a nut is rusted tight, cut through it with a hacksaw; the easiest way is to cut down, as shown, and then unscrew it. With a helper, lift the toilet off the flange and carry it to another room. Stuff a rag in the closet flange (make sure it's large enough so it won't fall down the hole) to contain sewer gases, and scrape off any wax, putty, or caulk.

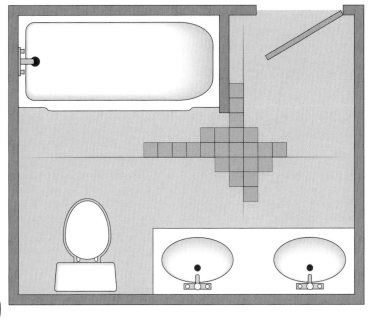

 LAY OUT THE JOB.

Small, rectangular bathroom floors are relatively easy to lay out. Arrange grout joints so they are parallel to the most visible straight edges in the room, such as along counters and tubs. Hide cut tiles in less exposed spots. In such a small area, it is worth your while to check the layout by dry-setting all of the tiles before you begin the installation. See pages 123–125.

SET THE TILES.

Set full tiles as close as possible to the closet flange. Use nippers to cut tiles to fit around the flange. Don't worry about precision here, because the toilet will cover the area.

RESET THE TOILET.

After the tile has been set and grouted, reset the toilet. Install new bolts in the flange; they may need to be longer than the old ones. Clean the horn of the bowl and set a rope of plumbers putty around it. Install a new wax ring. If the flange is well below the finished tile surface, you may need a second wax ring to seal the gap. Set the toilet over the bolts and tighten the nuts.

TILING OVER TILE

When remodeling a bathroom, you may consider covering an old tiled floor with new tiling. Removing the old tile can be a major headache, but it may not be necessary. You can use the existing floor as a setting bed for the new tile, if conditions are right

First make certain there are no structural problems with the floor—if the grout is significantly cracked and tiles are loose, it could signal underlying problems that need to be addressed before proceeding. Talk to your tile dealer about the best products and techniques to use over a tiled floor. Normally the old tiles will need to be sanded heavily to rough up the glazed surface. You may also need to fill in old grout joints if they aren't level with the tile surface.

Keep in mind the new tile will add to the height of your bathroom floor. Place tiles on top of your existing floor to find out whether this new height will make it awkward to move from the hall into the bathroom. Usually a threshold will smooth the transition.

Most professional tile setters agree that the best substrate for tile is an old-fashioned mortar bed. But laying it smooth is a job for the pros. Backerboard has made it easier for do-it-yourselfers to install their own tile. There are times, though, when backerboard won't work, such as when you cannot afford to raise the height of the finished floor too much. Entryways frequently pose this dilemma, because the floor connects with several rooms and often a stairway as well. In those situations a modified mortar-bed installation is best.

YOU'LL NEED

TIME: 2–4 days, depending on the size of the entryway and amount of preparation needed for the subfloor. Allow time for cement to cure.

SKILLS: Troweling cement to a consistent thickness, preparing a subfloor, tiling a floor.

TOOLS: Steel trowel, tiling and grouting tools.

BRINGING THE OUTDOORS IN

Often the best types of tile to use for an entryway are those commonly used on exterior applications, such as unglazed pavers (machine-made or handmade), slate, and half brick. If you also plan to tile an adjacent patio, porch, or other entrance to the house, use matching tiles inside and out to unify the spaces. Be sure the tiles you choose won't become slippery when wet.

1 PREPARE FLOOR.

Stabilize any spongy areas of the floor using drywall screws twice as long as the thickness of your flooring. If necessary add plywood so your subfloor totals at least $1\frac{1}{8}$ inches in thickness. Install 15-pound felt roofing paper overlapping the edges 2 to 3 inches, and staple the paper to the subfloor every 6 to 8 inches. After stapling trim the edges so the felt doesn't ride up any adjacent molding or stairs.

2 ATTACH METAL LATH.

Staple galvanized metal lath (mesh) over the felt paper. Available at masonry supply stores and large home centers in 2-foot-wide strips, the lath can be cut with tin snips. Butt the pieces together; don't overlap them.

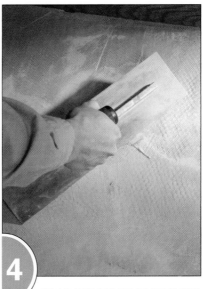

3 SPREAD THE MORTAR.

Prepare a cement mixture of half portland cement and half fine (builder's) sand. The fine sand should not contain stones that would make the surface bumpy. Spread cement with a steel trowel to a depth of ¼ inch, smoothing all ridges. Avoid smearing mortar on the stair riser or adjacent molding.

4 SMOOTH THE SURFACE.

Let the mortar cure overnight. Then carefully go over the cement with a trowel to scrape away any high spots. Sweep the surface to remove loose material.

5 LAY OUT AND SET TILES.

An entryway can be difficult to lay out, because different parts of the floor are visible from different directions. Choose the most public point of view and plan your layout around it. Dry-fit the tiles to ensure there won't be any slivers of tile.

6 GROUT AND SEAL.

If the tiles were not sealed when you bought them, apply the sealer recommended by the tile maker before grouting. After the tiles are set and grouted (see pages 142–144), wait about a week before applying a liquid top coat, which should be renewed once or twice a year.

CHOOSING SEALERS AND FINISHES

Grout lines, unglazed tile, and unpolished natural stone are vulnerable to stains, dirt, grease, and mildew. For protection of porous surfaces, apply a sealer or finish (the terms are interchangeable). Product types vary according to porosity of the material being covered and the degree of sheen you want. All require that the surface is clean, dry, and free from any other coatings or wax before application. Typically sealers and finishes can be applied in one coat, but for very porous surfaces such as brick, two coats are needed. Confirm that the sealer or finish you choose is rated for outdoor use; some are rated for indoor use only. Use a small paintbrush when sealing the grout alone; apply it with a roller when sealing tile and grout.

TILING STAIRS

The design of a stairway can set the tone of your home as you enter, or even help make a transition from one room to the next. However it is not a space where practicality should be compromised by design. Stairs receive a lot of foot traffic, and typically dirt and moisture accompany that traffic and can wear down the tread. Using tile provides a durable alternative tread surface. Tiles will protect against moisture, are easy to clean, and will withstand years of use.

Research shows that 95 percent of accidents that happen inside the home are falling accidents, so select a heavy-duty, slip-resistant tile with a bullnose front for the tread. Unglazed tiles typically offer better traction than glazed, but some glazed tiles have a more abrasive texture that might work. You can also use unglazed paver tiles similar to what you may use on outdoor steps. If you have questions about using tile on a stairway, don't hesitate to consult with your supplier. A nice combination is to use heavy-duty tiles on the tread and glazed, decorative tiles on the stair risers.

A simple way to add character to your stairway is to decorate the stair risers with bold and colorful accents. See Tiling Indoor Stair Risers (page 47).

∧

STAIR RISER CREATIVITY
The dark mosaic tiles, accenting the stair risers, add a contrasting element to the neutral tiles used on the walls and built-in tub. Using the same mosaic pattern on both the stair risers and the border gives the space a cohesive look. See page 47 for step-by-step instructions on tiling stair risers.

SECURE TILES

To help hold the tiles in place while the thinset mortar cures, you can either remove the bottom of a spacer and insert it between the tile and the tread, or insert a nail beneath the tile. Remove the spacer or nail once the thinset mortar has cured.

TILING INDOOR STAIR RISERS

Create a dramatic look on stairs by tiling only the risers. As shown in this project, ceramic tiles are a fabulous complement to hardwood treads. Stair risers are highly visible, and you can exercise a lot of creativity in mixing various colors or patterns. For example you can apply the same pattern across each stair consistently up the stairway. Or you can apply a solid tile to one row of stairs, and a pattern to the next, alternating all the way up the stairway. When selecting your tiles, remember to consider the colors and style of the entryway that leads to the staircase, as well as the space at the top of the stairs. The treads should overhang the risers by about an inch. If they do not, consult with a professional on how to adjust the tread. Use a bullnose radius tile to cover the edges of risers that are exposed and do not adjoin a wall.

YOU'LL NEED

TIME: 2–4 days. 1–2 days to lay the tiles, 24 hours to cure, and 1 day to grout and caulk.

SKILLS: Installing backerboard, using a wet saw, setting tiles, grouting and caulking.

TOOLS: Tape measure, screws, wet saw, rubber mallet and beating block, grouting, tiling and caulking tools.

1 MEASURE THE RISER.

Measure the riser and cut a strip of concrete backerboard ½ inch shorter than the riser. Attach it to the riser with screws, leaving a ¼-inch gap at the top and bottom. Also tape a piece of cardboard on the tread to protect it from the thinset mortar.

2 CUT THE TILES.

Dry-set with full tiles to plan any cuts. Using a wet saw, cut the tiles so there is a ⅛-inch gap at the top and bottom, to leave space for the caulk. Apply one row of full-size tiles across, or two rows of medium-size tiles, cutting the top row to fit.

3 SET THE TILES.

Back-butter the tiles before laying them. (It's easier to do this when working in a small space.) Set the tile firmly on the riser. Use a rubber mallet and beater block to gently tap the tiles into place.

4 GROUT AND CAULK.

When the thinset mortar has cured (wait 24 hours), grout the vertical seams. Treads will flex over time, therefore, to protect the tiles from cracking, use caulk in the tread seams.

TILING AN ENTRYWAY AREA PATTERN

A beautifully tiled entryway can make a strong design statement. The entryway is an introduction to your home, so keep the style of adjoining rooms in mind when designing the layout. Focus on keeping the entryway interesting without creating visual confusion. With a wide variety of tiles available, you can experiment with combinations of different-size tiles to create a unique effect. Remember that the entryway should also remain practical, able to stand up to heavy traffic, dirt, and moisture. Organized patterns require planning. Keep in mind the size of the space, the size of the pattern, and the size of the tiles. Spend time drawing different ideas on graph paper, and make sure you take the time to properly educate yourself about your suppliers' samples, knowing all of the sizes, colors, and finishes available for your design.

YOU'LL NEED

TIME: 2–4 days, depending on the amount of work put into predesigning the pattern. Time includes letting the tiles set before foot traffic is allowed.

SKILLS: Dry-setting tile, tiling an entryway, using a wet saw.

TOOLS: Graph paper, ruler, pencil, chalk line, rubber mallet and beater block, trowel, wet saw, tiling and grouting tools.

DISTINCTIVE PATTERNS.

This unique area-rug design is the result of a carefully planned layout of various sizes, shapes, and colors. Integrating a design into your floor layout can make a statement, create a theme, or even add practicality; but the most important step in executing a detailed pattern is drawing out the design in advance. This step will reveal any flaws in the design before you set the tiles. Experiment with different ideas until you come up with the one that best fits your style.

1 DRAW YOUR DESIGN.

It is important to plan the layout of the tiles. Pick up some graph paper from your local stationery store, and carefully draw your design. Fill in the different shapes, using colored pencils to show color variations. This will save you a lot of time and help to ensure that the tiles are positioned correctly the first time around.

2 MEASURE AND CHALK THE FLOOR.

To find the center of the space, attach a chalk line at the center of two opposite walls. Tighten and lift the chalk line, and let it "snap" onto the floor. Repeat the process on the other two opposite walls. The chalk line left behind will give you the center point of the space.

3 DRY-SET THE PATTERN.

When incorporating a defined pattern of tiles into your design, it is important to prepare a dry run to reveal any design flaws, so you can make necessary changes. If needed adjust the size of the pattern by cutting the tiles.

4 SET THE BORDER TILES.

Now that the field tiles are set, mark and cut your border tiles. See page 137 for tips on measuring and cutting border tiles. If the border area is small and you can not easily use your trowel to apply the adhesive, back-butter the tiles before setting them.

5 LAY OUT AND SET THE FIELD TILES.

Dry-set the field tiles to prevent any slivers of tile on the border. Adjust your layout accordingly. Prepare thinset mortar and set the tiles with spacers. Use a rubber mallet and beater block to even out the surface of the tiles. It's a good idea to check the adhesion about every 10 minutes to make sure the thinset mortar adheres to the entire surface.

6 SET THE CENTER TILES AND GROUT.

Finally set your pattern of tiles. Follow the instructions on page 136 for setting tiles. If you want to emphasize the pattern, choose a grout color that matches the main color of the tile. See page 142 for grouting techniques.

STAY OFF THE TILES

It is important not to walk on your freshly laid tiles right away. Stay off of them for at least a day—it's best to let them set overnight. Because the entryway is a high-traffic area, put up signs or barriers reminding others in the household to stay off the area.

You can use tile to create a functional, long-lasting, low-maintenance wall covering in any room you like. What really sets tile apart from other materials and coatings used on walls is the endless creative potential it offers. With floor tiles you are concerned about performance—sustaining heavy loads, holding up to scruffy shoes, not getting too slippery, and permitting easy cleaning. When choosing wall tiles your focus can shift to color, pattern, texture, and variety. With the exception of large, heavy tiles, virtually any tile available— handmade or factory-produced— can be set on a wall. In addition, window sills, backsplashes, tub surrounds, soffits, stove vents, and even cabinet doors can be tiled. The only limitation is that the substrate should be solid enough so it doesn't flex and crack the grout or tiles.

CHARMING DURABILITY
Tile is one of the few materials that can withstand the heat and grime around a stove while being delightfully decorative.

ORNATE BEAUTY
Beautifully detailed field and border tiles, such as the ones used in this ornate backsplash, can often be found at specialty tile stores or larger home centers. However if the tile you want is not in stock, check manufacturers' catalogs at your local retailer, or contact tile manufacturers directly for literature. Handmade tiles may be a little more difficult to find; they are typically sold at specialty tile retailers and at stores that feature locally produced crafts.

SUBTLE ANGLES

By framing an angled field of wall tiles with border tiles, you can install an attractive and easy-to-maintain surface behind your stove and sink areas. Setting the tiles diagonally breaks the monotony of a tiled wall and sets the wall treatment apart from that used on the countertops. Neutral colors keep the effect subtle.

UNIQUE DECORATIVES

Tile showrooms often carry a variety of decorative tiles, such as these border tiles. Local artisans can also be a great source for unique designs. Such specialty tiles as the ones surrounding this bathtub can be expensive. Fortunately you need only a few of them to create a noticeable effect.

In reality anyone can decorate a tile. Plain or off-white glazed ceramic tiles, paintbrushes, and some water-based ceramic paints are all you need to get started. Create patterns with stencils, or apply paint by dabbing sponges on the tile.

TILING WALLS

Walls often are not truly flat. Flexible drywall can be installed over bowed and twisted studs; when it is covered with paint or wallpaper, most people won't notice. If you try to install tile on an irregular wall, however, the underlying problem will be magnified. An out-of-plumb wall can be tiled, but it may affect the appearance of adjoining surfaces. If problems are severe, you're better off not installing tile.

YOU'LL NEED

TIME: About 1 hour per 5 square feet to set and grout tile, plus time for wall preparation.

SKILLS: Checking walls for straightness and squareness, preparing a substrate, installing tile, grouting.

TOOLS: Level, straightedge, tiling and grouting tools.

1 PREPARE THE WALLS.

Use a carpenter's level to check walls for plumb. Set a long level or straightedge against the wall at various points to determine if the wall is flat. Corners are especially important. Use thinset or patching plaster to fill depressions. Patch cracks and holes and repair any damaged areas in drywall or plaster

WALL SUBSTRATES

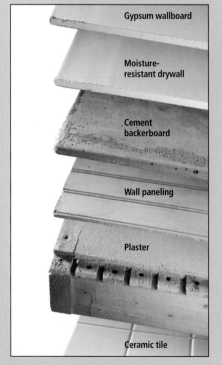

Gypsum wallboard

Moisture-resistant drywall

Cement backerboard

Wall paneling

Plaster

Ceramic tile

Tile can be installed over most existing wall surfaces as long as the wall is flat and in sound condition.

Gypsum wallboard. The most common wall surface, and a good substrate for tile in dry locations. Can also be used in moderately wet areas if you brush on liquid waterproofing before tiling. Repair holes or cracks with patching compound. Remove wallpaper and loose paint. Lightly sand painted surfaces. Perhaps add a second layer of drywall for added strength or to cover damaged areas.

Moisture-resistant drywall. Commonly known as greenboard or blueboard, it is similar to standard drywall, but is water-resistant—though not waterproof. It can be used in fairly wet areas, but should receive the same waterproofing installation as regular drywall.

Cement backerboard. An ideal substrate for tile, especially as part of a waterproof installation on shower walls or bathtub surrounds. When installing backerboard over an existing wall surface, use corrosion-resistant nails or screws long enough to penetrate the wall studs.

Wall paneling. Most sheet paneling is too thin and fragile to be used as a substrate for tile. Remove the paneling and cover the wall with backerboard or drywall before tiling.

Plaster. Install tile over plaster only if it is hard, flat, and in good condition. If the plaster crumbles when you poke it with a knife, it is too weak and should be replaced with backerboard or drywall. Repair cracks and indentations.

Ceramic tile. You can tile directly over a previously tiled surface as long as it is in good condition. Remove loose or broken tile and fill the cavity with mortar. Aggressively sand the surface to rough up the glaze.

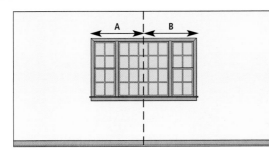

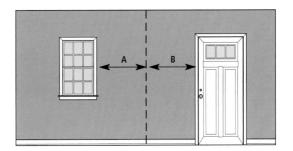

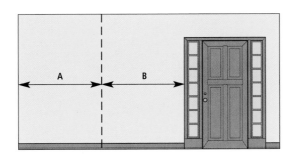

2 ESTABLISH A CENTERLINE AND REFERENCE LINES.

On a large wall, it is usually best to start the layout with a vertical line somewhere near the middle. If a single obstruction, such as a wall or a window, is reasonably centered in the room, then draw a line through its center. With two obstructions, make your centerline at the middle of the distance between their inside edges. If you have a single offset obstruction, divide the unobstructed portion of the wall in half. Then add a horizontal line to divide the wall into four quadrants. Add reference lines to separate the field tiles from any trim tiles. Use a carpenter's level to establish vertical and horizontal reference lines. On a wall less than 8 feet wide, you may want to make sure the cut tiles on either side are close to the same size. The only way to ensure this is to dry-set a complete horizontal course.

EXTENDING ELECTRICAL BOXES

When tiling around electrical outlets and switches, remove the coverplates and set tile right up to the cutout in the wall. This may mean that you will have to move the electrical box out, so it will be flush with the finished tile surface. Extension rings are available at electrical supply stores; mount them on the existing boxes. Before you begin tiling, make sure you find extension rings in the size you need, or talk to an electrician about other options.

3 HOLD THE TILES.

Gravity works against you when installing wall tiles. Usually wall tile adhesive is sticky enough so the tiles will not fall off, and most wall tiles are self-spaced, so they will not slide down. In a more difficult installation, you may have to use spacers to keep the tiles from slipping, and masking tape to hold them on the wall. On each column of tiles, affix tape that is taut and well-adhered to the wall tile while the adhesive cures.

COPING WITH OBSTRUCTIONS

A careful do-it-yourselfer can usually produce professional-looking results when tiling a flat, unobstructed wall. Handling those not-so-flat walls full of obstructions is more difficult. You'll have to plan carefully if your project entails working around obstacles or turning corners. Learning how to anticipate such disruptions is a necessary component of every installation. One approach—and often the wisest—is simply to avoid obstructions whenever possible. And for those times when you can't ignore the obstruction, tackle it head on. Practice cutting and trimming tiles so the act becomes almost second nature.

IDEAL SETTING
If a window is set in a deep recess, consider tiling the sill and perhaps the sides as well. A tiled window surround makes an ideal setting for potted plants.

INTERESTING ANGLES
Sometimes obstructions create opportunities for interesting designs. Rather than tiling the entire wall behind this stove (and having to make cutouts for receptacles) this angled arrangement bypasses them.

PLUMBING PROFICIENCY
Installing tile in a bathroom will often involve working around existing plumbing pipes, drains, and fixtures. Sometimes you can handle the problem by dismantling the plumbing, cutting or drilling a hole in the tile before installing it (see page 127), and then replacing the plumbing after the tile is in place. Other times you must work around the plumbing, notching the tile as needed (see page 135).

ELECTRICAL EXPERTISE

Electrical fixtures, receptacles, and switches such as the ones in this bathroom are common obstructions that look deceptively easy to work around. The main difficulty is extending the metal or plastic fixture, switch, or receptacle box so it is flush with the finished tile surface. Purchase easy-to-install box extenders for the electrical box. When these are in place, trim tile to wrap around the box (see pages 53 and 135).

CAREFUL PLANNING

Major appliances such as this commercial-grade cooktop and vent take special planning. Manufacturer's specifications are helpful, but there is no substitute for having the unit itself on hand to confirm measurements when tiling. Plan your installation so the cooktop can be readily removed without damaging the tile.

CORNER PROTECTION

Corners are the most commonly encountered obstruction in tiling. Lay out your job carefully so the horizontal grout joints on adjacent walls are aligned. Outside corners are vulnerable to damage. Plastic trim pieces can be used to protect the edge.

A tiled window recess won't rot, will prevent and resist water stains, and won't get scratched by cats seeking a sunny refuge. Terracotta tiles are an attractive choice; decorative, hand-painted tiles can add a splash of color.

If the surrounding wall is tiled, incorporate the window recess into the larger project. Use bullnose tiles or special windowsill tiles to round the edges. It is usually best to tile the recess after the wall, so the recess tiles can overlap the wall tile. In a tub surround with a window, cut down on maintenance problems by replacing sashes with glass block and then tiling the recess.

YOU'LL NEED

TIME: 1–2 days. Less than a day of labor, but allow 1 day for the adhesive to cure before grouting.

SKILLS: Removing molding, setting wall tile.

TOOLS: Flat pry bar, tiling and grouting tools.

TILE AS TRIM

Tile can make a stunning impact when it is used for small accents. One excellent example: Wood casing trim around doors and windows serves to hide an unattractive gap between materials. Tile can perform that function just as well, and with a good deal more pizzazz, especially if you choose decorative trim tiles.

1 REMOVE MOLDING AND SILL.

Remove the window casing, then pry off the sill. You may need to cut the sill to get it out. Then examine the jamb, and decide how far inward toward the window the tile will extend. If the window has stop molding, decide whether to leave it in place or remove it. Install backerboard on top of the jamb.

2 PREPARE THE WALL.

Stuff the gap with fiberglass insulation if none is present; on an old window take care not to hinder the movement of the sash ropes and weights. If you will be tiling the wall, apply fiberglass mesh joint tape, and fill in with joint compound. Allow it to dry, apply a second coat, and sand smooth. If you will be painting the wall, carefully install metal outside of the corner bead, apply joint compound, and sand. Sand the jamb as well.

3 SUPPORT TOP PIECES.

Install any wall tiles flush to the jamb, so you will have a consistent grout line at the corners (see right). Make a support system using three boards to hold the ceiling tiles in place. Allow them to set before continuing.

4 SET THE TILES.

Set tiles in adhesive and grout the same as for a standard wall installation. Use bullnose pieces for a tiled wall (as shown) or for a painted wall. Or use one of the other options pictured below.

5 CAULK THE WINDOW.

Take special care to completely caulk the joint between the tile and the window to prevent water damage.

OTHER CORNER OPTIONS.

The arrangement shown in the steps above, with bullnose pieces used on the recessed surfaces, is the most common to tile a window recess (see Step 4). You may, however, use bullnose pieces on the wall . Or use corner edging tiles similar to V-cap tiles used on countertops (left). Install the edging pieces before tiling the recess. For a decorative touch, apply a border strip around the recess (right). Install bullnose pieces in the recess so they cap the border strips, or butt field tiles up to the border pieces, if they have a finished edge.

TILING COUNTERTOPS

Tile countertops are durable and offer a wide range of color and texture options that can make them an attractive design feature. However be aware that tile is much more prone to break dropped glasses and dishes than are other countertop surfaces. In addition grout stains easily and can be tough to clean, even if coated with a grout sealer.

To keep up appearances, choose colors and materials that won't show stains, and keep the countertop clean and well maintained. Dark-colored glazes are more likely to show scratches than light-colored glazes. Glazed, vitreous, or impervious tiles do the best job of resisting moisture and stains.

TILE SELECTIVELY

Some people don't want to consider tile for countertop use, at least in the kitchen, because of its hard surface and the difficulty of keeping grout joints clean. However you can use tile and avoid most of these problems by being selective. Don't install tile on the major food preparation surfaces in the kitchen. Instead match the material used on the surface with the function of the countertop. Plastic laminate, for example, might be preferred around the sink and food preparation area, while tile can cover other countertops in the kitchen. Or save the tile for use only as a backsplash.

CAUTIOUS INSTALLATION
For a band of dramatic color and a practical surface, run your countertop tile up onto the backsplash. Use tile, adhesive, and grout that can withstand moisture. Install the tiles over a membrane and backerboard (see pages 116–118) to assure that your project will withstand the hard use a kitchen demands.

BOLD CONTRASTS
One of the distinct pleasures of tiling a bathroom is you can feel free to be a bit playful. Experiment with playful colors and bold patterns you wouldn't think about using in any other room. Make a small bathroom feel larger by using splashes of color, or give the room a unified sense by sticking to a single color throughout.

TILE VERSATILITY

Tile has always been more popular in the bathroom than in the kitchen because you don't have to worry about the aesthetic and hygienic effects of food and grease spills, or breaking fragile dishes on the hard surface. Because tile is so often used elsewhere in the bath, it makes sense to use it on the countertop as well.

STRENGTH AND DURABILITY

There are advantages to using tile around a cooktop. Heat generated by the burners will not affect the tiles, and most tiles won't be damaged if you place a hot pan on them. Often it makes sense to use tile around the cooktop and use other surfacing materials for countertops in the sink and food preparation areas.

LAYING OUT COUNTERTOPS

Countertops are everyday work surfaces, and are often subject to up-close scrutiny. Small misalignments can grow into major distractions if you have to stare at them all the time, so take the time to get your layout perfect. Most countertops are small enough that you can do a full dry run with loose tiles before starting the installation. Try to place equal-size cut tiles along the sides and back. If the back wall is uneven, make the adjustment with the cut tiles at the back.

YOU'LL NEED

TIME: 1½ days to install substrate and tile.

SKILLS: Measuring and marking a layout, cutting and fastening plywood.

TOOLS: Drill, level, square, circular saw or jigsaw.

1 INSTALL A PLYWOOD SURFACE.

The countertop substrate should be at least one layer of ¾-inch plywood. Take care that the front edges are square and parallel to the walls. Make the whole top perfectly level. Attach with construction adhesive and screws.

USING AN EXISTING COUNTERTOP AS THE SUBSTRATE

If conditions are right, you can tile over an existing laminated countertop. The top must be square edged; a countertop with rounded edges will not work. And it must be in sound condition, level, and firmly connected to the cabinets.

Remove the backsplash. Sand the entire surface thoroughly—use an electric vibrating sander, or spend a good deal of time hand-sanding with a sanding block and 60-grit sandpaper.

2 WATERPROOF THE SUBSTRATE.

For a fully waterproofed installation, add a waterproofing membrane (15-pound felt paper or 4-mil polyethylene) followed by cement backerboard. Seal the joints of the backerboard with fiberglass mesh tape, filled with thinset mortar.

3 LAY OUT THE JOB.

When laying out an L-shape countertop, start at the inside corner, and plan to use full tiles there. Align field tiles with the edge of the substrate, unless you use edging trim tiles, in which case draw a reference line separating trim from field tiles. (See page 63 for edging possibilities.) If possible plan so grout lines will be evenly spaced from the sides of the sink. Run cut tiles around the back edges, along the backsplash.

4 MARK THE SINK CUTOUT.

Determine where the sink can fit into your sink base cabinet. Flip the sink upside down and trace the outline. Remove the sink and draw a cut line about 1 inch inside the outline. Some new sinks come with a paper template that can be used instead.

5 CUT THE HOLE.

You could cut the opening with a circular saw, starting with a plunge cut, but cutting through backerboard with a circular saw will make a huge cloud of dust, so use a jigsaw instead. Drill holes just inside the cut line at each corner, using a drill bit large enough to match the radius of the sink corners. Use a jigsaw equipped with a rough-cutting blade to cut the sink opening; have extra blades on hand. Install the sink before or after tiling, depending on the type of sink (see below).

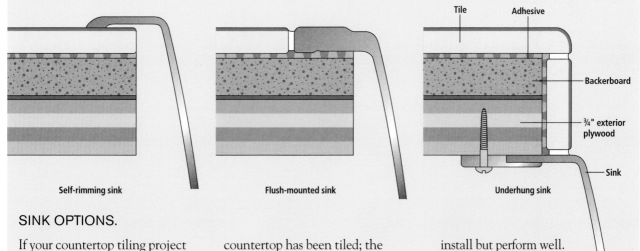

Self-rimming sink   **Flush-mounted sink**   **Underhung sink**

Labels on diagram: Tile, Adhesive, Backerboard, ¾" exterior plywood, Sink

SINK OPTIONS.

If your countertop tiling project involves a sink, be sure to buy the sink and learn how it is installed before you set any tile. The most common type of kitchen sink is self-rimming. Install it after the countertop has been tiled; the edges of the sink rest on top of the tile. Install a flush-mounted sink before tiling, and run the tile up to the edge of the sink. Underhung sinks are slightly more difficult to install but perform well. Flush-mounted and underhung sinks don't have a lip, so messes and water from the countertop can be wiped directly into the sink.

SETTING TILE COUNTERTOPS

Choose tiles made for the purpose. That usually means they will be ¼- or ³⁄₁₆-inch thick. They should be glazed to prevent them from staining easily. It is usually best to use either a light-colored grout or one that comes close to the color of the tile, rather than a dark, starkly contrasting color that will emphasize any imperfections.

To be sure the tile color and finish are consistent, work with a tile dealer who can supply you with all of the field tiles, decorative or bullnose tiles for the front edge, and radius bullnose for the backsplash. Every tile with an exposed side must have a rounded edge (called a bullnose) or a cap. Don't use a field tile and then attempt to give it a finished edge with grout; it will look ugly and wear poorly.

Choose the adhesive recommended by your dealer. Thinset mortar is usually the best choice. If you want to make the installation waterproof, be sure to choose all materials with that in mind.

Work slowly and systematically. Setting a tile countertop is an ideal weekend project, and provides good training for tackling more complex tiling jobs later on.

YOU'LL NEED

TIME: 1–2 days. A full day to install about 12 feet of countertop, plus 2–3 hours the following day for grouting and cleaning.

SKILLS: Dry-setting, spreading adhesive; cutting, installing, and grouting tile.

TOOLS: Tape measure, level, square, tile cutter, notched trowel, hammer, beater block, grout float.

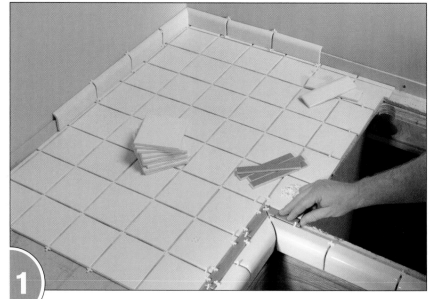

1 PLAN THE JOB.

Prepare a firm, level, and flat surface for the tiles. Be sure the total thickness of the substrate will be covered by the edging you choose (see page 63). Check the substrate for level and square. If you are using backsplash edging tile with a large radius, provide backing for it by fastening a strip of backerboard to the wall (see page 131). Check the layout for the backsplash to find out if you will encounter any obstructions.

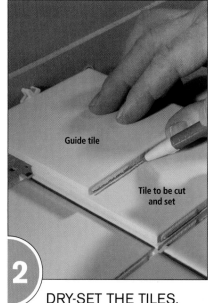

Guide tile

Tile to be cut and set

2 DRY-SET THE TILES.

Set the tiles in place, positioning them exactly as you want the finished surface to look. Use plastic spacers and check that all lines are straight. To mark lines for cutting, use a tile as a guide rather than measuring (see page 137).

THE RIGHT GROUT

Because grout joints on countertops are visible and subjected to spills, it is important to use the best grout mixture possible. Use sanded grout for grout joints wider than ¹⁄₁₆ inch. Mix the grout with a liquid latex additive rather than water for added protection against liquid penetration. If mildew is likely to be a problem, use an additive that inhibits the growth of mildew. Plan to seal the grout a week or two after installation.

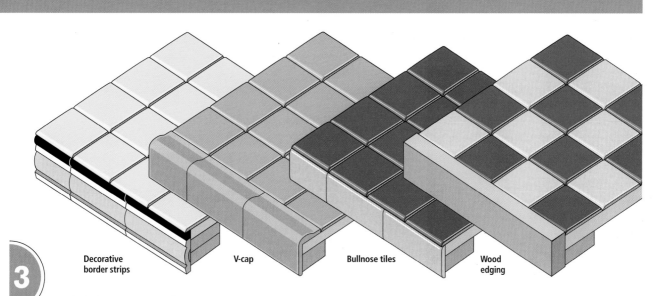

Decorative border strips   V-cap   Bullnose tiles   Wood edging

3 CHOOSE THE EDGING.

The edging on a countertop is not just a decorative element added on at the end of the job. As an integral part of the counter, it must figure in your planning at each step. Your choice of edge treatment will affect preparation and thickness of the substrate as well as the placement of reference lines.

You can add color and interest to a countertop by edging it with a combination of decorative border strips overlapped by bullnose tiles. A V-cap provides a slight lip that keeps water from dripping down the edge of the counter. Another alternative involves two bullnose edging pieces, one on the counter surface, one on the edging. Install the edge pieces and the surface tiles at the same time to keep them aligned.

EDGING WITH WOOD

Wood looks great as an edging material on kitchen countertops, and it is easy to install. It does create some additional maintenance concerns, however. Wood expands and contracts with temperature and humidity changes, but tile and grout do not. Keep the wood separated from the tile with caulk. Set the edging flush with the top of the tile, or a little higher to create a drip-proof lip. Position the tiles about ⅛ inch shy of the edge of the substrate, to allow space for caulk. Attach the edging to the plywood substrate with countersunk screws every 6 to 8 inches, then hide the screw heads with plugs. Or attach the edging with biscuit joints, for a surface free from screw holes.

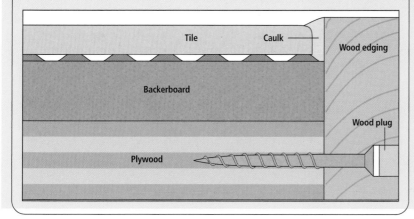

Tile   Caulk   Wood edging

Backerboard

Wood plug

Plywood

CAUTION

SEAL THE WOOD

One of the biggest challenges posed by wood edging on a countertop is keeping the wood looking as good as new years after it was installed. Use a tough hardwood, such as maple or oak, to help minimize dents and scrapes. Before installing the edging, coat all sides with a durable clear wood finish such as polyurethane. Apply more finish to any penetrations made in the wood while it is being installed. In the years to come, watch for dark stains on the wood, which could indicate that water found its way into the wood. In that case sand away the stain and apply another coat of finish.

Setting tile countertops *(continued)*

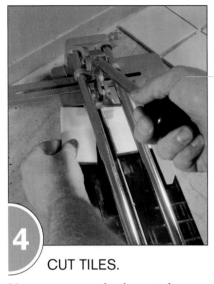

4 CUT TILES.

Use a snap cutter for the straight cuts. Many will be for the same size pieces, so set the guide and make multiple cuts before resetting. For small curved or irregular cuts, use nippers or a rod saw. For large projects a wet saw will make the cutting work go faster. See pages 134–135 for instructions.

5 SPREAD ADHESIVE.

Mix the thinset mortar as directed on the label. If the powder does not contain a latex additive, use a liquid additive instead of water to mix with the powder. Let the mixture rest for 10 minutes, then mix it again. Spread the adhesive with a notched trowel.

6 SET TILES.

Set the tiles along the reference lines, pressing each one into the adhesive with a slight twist. Avoid sliding the tiles. Use plastic spacers to keep all of the joints even. Check the alignment of set tiles regularly.

BACKSPLASH OPTIONS

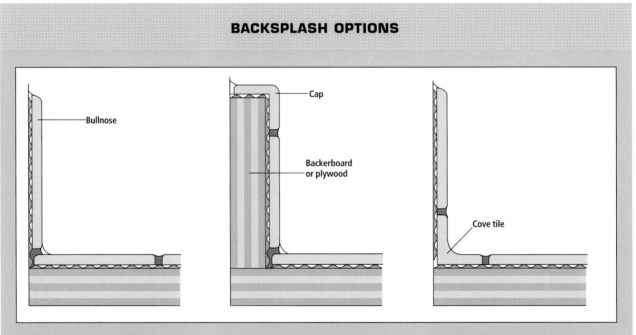

Bullnose

Cap

Backerboard or plywood

Cove tile

Integrate the backsplash with the countertop by using the same tiles on both surfaces with grout joints that line up. Or treat the backsplash as an element all its own, using colors and sizes of tile that are unrelated to those on the countertop. Make colorful backsplashes by using a variety of tiles. If you are setting backsplash tiles directly on the wall, it must be flat and in sound condition. Use standard bullnose tiles (caps). A built-up backsplash mimics the look of a traditional mortar-bed installation. Use plywood or cement backerboard to fill in the space behind a radius bullnose. A cove tile in the corner makes cleanup easier. Each material requires a different layout.

7 BED THE TILES.

After setting tiles in one section, bed them into the adhesive with a beater block. Move the beater block over the tiles while tapping lightly with a hammer. Clean out any excess adhesive that squeezes into grout joints.

8 SET BACKSPLASH TILES.

If you are using backsplash tiles the same width as the tiles on the countertop, install them so the grout joints line up. These tiles are not subjected to much wear and tear, so it is possible to set them directly on the wall. Set backsplash tiles above the countertop tiles by the width of a grout joint.

9 TRIM THE BACKSPLASH.

If you use bullnose tiles set directly on the wall, you will not need to add trim tiles to the backsplash. If the backsplash is built out away from the wall, add radius bullnose trim tiles.

10 GROUT AND SEAL.

Let the tiles set for 24 hours. Mix grout with a latex additive. Apply with a grout float, pushing the mixture into the joints. When the joints are filled, hold the float at nearly a right angle to the countertop and wipe away the excess. Do not use grout in the joint between the countertop and backsplash tiles; this joint and the space between the backsplash tile and the wall should be filled with caulk or sealant. Wipe away excess grout with a damp sponge, repeating often until the grout haze is gone. Apply grout sealer after the grout has cured.

TILING A MURAL BACKSPLASH

The kitchen is often the heart of the home, and over the years has become a place where families gather not only to enjoy meals, but also to talk, play, and even watch television. And during social gatherings it is also where guests tend to congregate.

With this in mind, the kitchen is a great place to establish the theme of your home. A decorative mural is a great way to create a focal point and enhance the current features of the space. Adding a mural to a kitchen backsplash makes practical sense too, as water-resistant tiles protect walls from water damage and other stains.

An ideal place for inserting a mural is above the stove or cooktop. Murals are usually created by putting together individually painted tiles into one cohesive picture. While planning be sure to take into consideration the colors surrounding where you will insert your mural.

YOU'LL NEED

TIME: 2–3 days. 1 day to set the tiles, 24 hours to cure, and another day to grout and seal.

SKILLS: Installing backerboard and tile, using a wet saw, dry-setting tile, caulking, grouting, and sealing.

TOOLS: Level, pencil, bucket and sponge, tape measure, rubber float, tile nippers, notched trowel, caulking tools.

DECORATIVE MURALS.

These decorative murals are built-up from individually painted tiles, creating one unified picture. Decorative murals allow you to express your personality and add that final, unique touch that makes this space stand out from the rest. Consider consulting with a local artist, or even painting your own tiles to add another level of interest to your project.

1 PREPARE THE WALL AND SET FIELD TILES.

Follow the instructions for installing backerboard on page 131. Measure the center of the stove or cooktop and make a pencil mark. Draw a vertical centerline up from the mark. This is your guide to position the mural to lay the first tile. Set the field tiles at the bottom of the vertical centerline. Leave about a ⅛-inch space at the bottom for the grout. Continue until you reach the space where the mural will be positioned.

2 SET THE MURAL TILES.

Dry-set the mural tiles to ensure that you have the piece or pieces cut to size. Apply thinset mortar to the mural area and set the tile. If applicable apply border tiles to the outside of the mural design.

3 SET THE SURROUNDING WALL TILES.

If necessary use a wet saw to cut any tiles that need to be notched around a cabinet corner or electrical outlet. Install bullnose tile at any open ends of the backsplash that do not butt up against a cabinet or adjoining wall. Once all of the tiles are set, apply caulk to the bottom of the backsplash, on inside corners, and between the tiles and cabinets.

Follow the instructions for applying grout and sealant on pages 142 and 148.

PROTECT YOURSELF

Safety is extremely important when doing any home improvement project, so it is a good idea to give some forethought to what might be a potential hazard in the room where you're working. In the kitchen drop cloths used to protect your stove or cooktop may present a potential fire hazard. Simply remove the knobs from your burners to prevent them from being accidentally turned on and catching the cloth on fire.

PERSONAL TOUCH

If your budget allows, hire an artist to design a custom mural for your home. Find a local artist who can visit your home and grasp the look and feel you want to create. Start with the phone book and contact the nearest art organization. Be sure to review several artists' work and commission one who understands your personal style and the type of mural you want for your home.

Glass tiles are impervious to stains and moisture, making them an ideal candidate for a kitchen backsplash. This is especially true behind the sink or work area, where the tiles can help protect the walls from water and other liquids that might splash up from blending or mixing. They add not only utility to the workspace but beauty as well. Glass tiles are often made from recycled goods, and their colors can be swirled, metallic, or even iridescent. Mosaics are small tiles that range from about ¾×¾ inch up to about 2×2 inches. Glass mosaics are typically mounted on a paper backing in larger pieces, for easy installation. If the glass tile is translucent, use a white thinset mortar, because the gray thinset mortar may show through and affect the clarity of the color. See page 138 for more information on installing mosaics.

YOU'LL NEED

TIME: 2–3 days. 1 day to set tiles, 24 hours to cure, and another day to grout and seal.

SKILLS: Assessing walls, installing backerboard, cutting tiles, applying grout.

TOOLS: Tape measure, level, tile cutter, hammer, notched trowel.

ADD SOME COLOR

Mosaic glass and other glass tiles are available in a wide range of colors, making them an ideal way to add a splash of color to an otherwise neutral kitchen. Consider pairing bold glass backsplash tiles with a natural-hue countertop, or choose vibrant colors for both surfaces for even more pizzazz.

BOLD PRACTICALITY.

This kitchen backsplash combines two colors of iridescent mosaic glass tiles to create a fun, bold look. White grout is used to ensure that the clarity of the mosaics is not affected. Glass tiles stand up to daily wear and tear, easily guarding against stains. See page 149 for tips on keeping white grout clean.

MOSAIC OPTIONS.

Glass mosaics offer up a variety of sizes, colors, and textures. As pictured here glass mosaics range from ¾×¾ inches to 2×2 inches, but these small tiles are usually mounted on a 12×12-inch paper backing for easy installation. They are impervious, making them an ideal choice for the wetter areas of your home.

1 ASSESS THE WALLS.

Set a long level or straightedge against the wall at various points to determine if the wall is flat. An uneven wall can be tiled, but it may affect the appearance of adjoining surfaces. If the wall is not reasonably flat, repair it first. Mark the perimeter of a depression with a pencil. Apply thinset with a trowel. Pay special attention to corners, where variations are most noticeable. Apply a skimcoat of thinset to bring adjacent surfaces to plumb.

2 SET THE TILES.

Prepare a dry run before setting tiles. Gravity works against you when installing wall tiles. Wall tile adhesive is usually sticky enough so the tiles will not fall off, and most wall tiles are self-spaced, so they will not slide down. In a more difficult installation, you may have to use spacers to keep the tiles from slipping, and masking tape to hold them on the wall. On each column of tiles, affix tape that is taut and bonded well to the wall tile while the adhesive cures.

3 APPLY THE FINISHING TOUCHES.

After the adhesive cures, follow the instructions on pages 142–144 for grouting. Consider using a grout that has a mildew-resistant compound that will prevent bacteria and food particles from collecting in the joints. If you are tiling behind a sink, use caulk to make a waterproof seal between the tiles and the sink.

KALEIDOSCOPE OF COLOR
The mix of swirled and iridescent mosaic glass tiles adorning this kitchen's countertop and backsplash forms a kaleidoscope of color, creating a focal point and no doubt a conversation piece. Their beauty is complemented by their water-shedding ability—a winning combination of form and function.

TILING A BATHROOM

There is no mistaking the practicality of installing tile in the bathroom—it is probably the wettest part of the house. The bathroom can be a place where a busy family starts each day, but it can also be a place of retreat and relaxation, where you wind down with a bubble bath. These goals are not opposites. You can create a functional space no matter what style you choose. As you plan your project, ask yourself a few questions: Who will be using the bathroom? What style do they prefer? Is creating a spalike environment important? If the bathroom is attached to a bedroom consider the style and color of the bedroom and choose complementary tiles.

If the bathroom is small, mirrors can help create a greater sense of space (see "Building a Mirror Tile Frame" on page 74). If there aren't any windows in the room, consider creating a new focal point with a mural of outdoor scenery. Place the mural opposite the mirror for maximum effect.

GEOMETRIC GENIUS
Glazed tiles on the sinktop and backsplash provide a practical bathroom surface. Impervious to water, the tiles will withstand years of use. The backsplash adds a creative touch by combining different shapes and colors to form a geometric design. The mirrors add depth to the space. See page 72 for tiling a bathroom sinktop.

SIMPLE ELEGANCE
You don't have to be elaborate to make a statement. The careful design of the mosaic floor gives this simple bathroom a bit of flair. Blue mosaics are layed out to form a small circle, resembling a flower. The blue-and-white-striped curtains highlight the design, without overpowering the space. See page 138 for details on setting mosaics.

CLASSIC CONTEMPORARY
This contemporary bathroom is designed with clean lines of gray stone tile. A dark border adds interest. The area rugs with black-and-white trim pull the design together. See page 78 for step-by-step instructions for tiling a tub surround.

TILING A BATHROOM SINKTOP

This project takes some time and patience, but the result can be a sinktop that adds an appealing custom touch to your makeover, melding the sink area with other tile surfaces in your bathroom.

Begin with an off-the-shelf cabinet base or, if you are an experienced woodworker, make one yourself. Select the sink, faucet, and grout at the same time you buy your tiles, so you have a grouping that goes well together. Avoid choosing a pigmented grout of a color that contrasts strongly with the tiles.

YOU'LL NEED

TIME: 1½ days to install substrate and tile.

SKILLS: Dry-setting tile, measuring and marking a layout, cutting and fastening plywood.

TOOLS: Drill, level, square, circular saw or jigsaw, tiling and grouting tools.

1 INSTALL THE CABINET.

If not already in place, install drain and supply lines. Cut holes in the back of the cabinet for the pipes, and slide in the cabinet. Shim at the floor and wall where necessary to ensure that the cabinet is plumb and level. Attach it to the wall by driving screws through the cabinet framing and into wall studs.

CHOOSING MATERIALS

Choose tiles that are made for the purpose; regular wall tiles will crack. The tiles you use should be ⅜- to ½-inch thick with a glazed surface. Buy all of the tiles at the same time, including the regular field tiles as well as the bullnose tiles for the edges of the counter and the backsplash.

A vitreous china sink is a compatible choice because its surface has a texture similar to tile. Enameled cast iron is also a good choice. A self-rimming sink is easiest to install; you can simply set it on top of the countertop and cover the rough edges of the cut tiles.

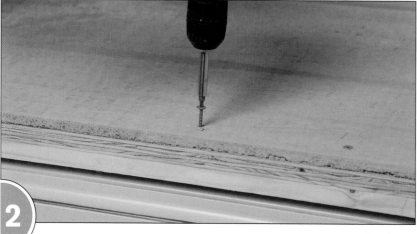

2 BUILD THE SUBSTRATE.

The surface under your tiles must be perfectly flat and smooth, and the edges and backsplash should be properly sized to accommodate your arrangement of bullnose tiles. Try to plan the size of the subsurface so you will use as many whole tiles as possible.

Cut ¾-inch plywood to the size needed. To thicken the substrate for tile edging, fasten 1×2 pieces around the perimeter of the cabinet with glue and screws. On top of the plywood, add a piece of cement backerboard. Attach it with screws, driving the heads just below the surface.

3 CUT THE HOLE.

The sink manufacturer may supply you with a template for marking the cutout. If not, center the sink upside down on the top of the backerboard and draw an outline. Draw a second line about ¾ inch inside the first, and cut that line with a jigsaw.

4 DRY-SET THE TILES.

Lay the tiles out exactly where you want them, using plastic spacers for all the joints and cutting tiles where necessary. When setting down pieces at the perimeter, remember that the mortar behind the edging pieces will be about ⅛-inch thick. Hold the sink in place above the opening to make sure no tile edges will be visible.

5 APPLY THE ADHESIVE.

Remove the tiles and place them in the order in which they will be adhered. Mix thinset mortar and apply it with a notched trowel by first laying it on thickly, then combing it with the notches for a perfectly level surface. Give the tiles a little push as you place them. Use the spacers to maintain consistent joint lines.

6 INSTALL THE SINK.

Grout the tiles, and allow the grout to dry. Set the sink in place, and make the plumbing connections. If the sink has mounting clips, install and tighten them; a heavy sink will not need them. Finish by running a bead of silicone caulk around the sink's rim. Smooth the caulk using a rag soaked with paint thinner.

REMOVING OLD SINKS.

Rimmed sinks are usually easy to remove: just unhook the plumbing connections, disconnect mounting clips (if any) from underneath, cut the bead of caulk, and pull the sink up from the countertop.

Other types of sinks require more work. If you cannot turn the countertop and sink upside down, be sure to support the sink as you remove it. Otherwise it may fall down into the cabinet. For an underhung sink (shown at right), or a flush-mounted sink, use a couple of pieces of 2×4 and a length of rope to support the sink as you remove the clamps that hold it in place. If the mounting clamps are rusted, use penetrating oil before unscrewing them.

If you want to keep your tiles and if your new sink will be large enough, carefully chip away the old quarter-round tiles that cover the top of a recessed sink so the surface tiles are preserved. Then install a self-rimming sink that covers the opening.

BUILDING A MIRROR TILE FRAME

Tiles are ideal in the bathroom for flooring, walls, tub surrounds, and even the bath and basin. The bathroom offers many opportunities to accessorize with accent tiles, decorating bathroom fixtures such as soap dishes, a shelf unit, or, as seen in this project, a bathroom mirror. Bathrooms are often small, and mirrors can create an illusion that the space is larger than it actually is. In this project border tiles frame the mirror. As an alternative you could use larger, full-size tiles if working with a full-length mirror. When choosing the border tiles for the mirror, try to work with what has already been used in another part of the bathroom. In this project the listellos used to frame the mirror are the same listellos used at the top of the wall tiles, tying together the design of the bathroom.

YOU'LL NEED

TIME: 2–3 days. 1 day to set the tiles, 24 hours to cure, and 1 day to grout and clean.

SKILLS: Tiling a wall, working with border tiles.

TOOLS: Pencil, straightedge, putty knife, grouting and sealing tools.

SMOOTH AND SUBTLE.

The thin listellos used at the top of the wall tiles are also used to frame the mirror acting as an accent piece that polishes off the look and provides visual interest to this monochromatic bathroom. The clean, simple lines of the listellos are smooth and rounded complimenting the shape of the bathroom sink and accessories.

1 CUT PLYWOOD.

Measure a piece of plywood and cut it to the size of the mirror plus the decorative tile border. First measure the width of the mirror. Next measure the width of the tile and multiply by 2, then add the two numbers. For example if the mirror is 12 inches wide, and the tile is 2 inches wide ($2 \times 2 = 4$ and $12 + 4 = 16$), the plywood should be cut into a 16×16-inch square. Next attach a 1-inch bevel-cut strip to the back of the plywood base.

2 PRIME THE PLYWOOD BASE.

To protect the plywood from moisture, and to prepare it for attaching the mirror and tile, prime the plywood using a general-purpose primer. Once it dries (about 4 hours), you are ready to set the mirror and tiles. For extra protection you can apply a second coat of primer about 16 hours after the initial application.

3 SET THE MIRROR.

Find the center of the plywood by drawing a straight line from opposite corners. Place the mirror in the center of the plywood and trace its exact location. Apply a waterproof mirror adhesive to the back of the mirror, and set the mirror onto the plywood.

NEW LIFE FOR AN OLD MIRROR

If you want to tile a mirror that is already affixed to the wall, measure your tiles and, using a level, mark where the tiles will be placed. Attach a supporting batten, and back-butter and set the bottom row of tiles. Continue applying the border tiles around the mirror until it is complete. To prevent the tiles on the sides of the mirror from moving out of alignment, attach temporary battens.

4 SET THE TILES.

Once the mirror is secure, prepare a dry run of the tiles around the mirror to make sure you won't have any awkward slivers. Since you're working in a small space, you may want to apply adhesive to the back of the tile and set each tile individually onto the plywood.

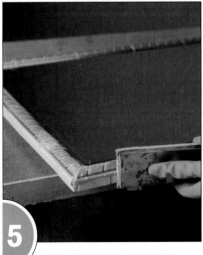

5 ADD THE FINISHING TOUCHES.

Clean any excess grout from the edges of the tiles and allow it to cure. After the grout has cured, follow the sealing instructions on page 148.

TILING SHOWERS AND TUBS

Perhaps nowhere else in the house does tile so successfully unite beauty and functionality as in the bath. Properly installed, tile can easily resist water. With so many colors, sizes, and patterns available, you are almost guaranteed to find a design that satisfies all of your needs. And when it comes time for cleanup, tile will demand less of your time than just about any other material. Perhaps best of all, it has never been easier for a do-it-yourselfer to accomplish professional-looking results. The secret to a long-lasting shower and tub installation is taking the extra effort to make the surface waterproof and performing the routine maintenance required to keep it that way.

BUILT-IN VERSATILITY
Few materials other than tile could successfully wrap the raised floor, built-in seat, and window of this oversized shower area.

SEAMLESS TRANSITION
Tile accommodates the custom profile of this corner bath, seamlessly merging with the glass-block step.

UNIFIED TRANSFORMATION

Tile is a natural material for waterproofing awkward spaces. In this bathroom tile helps transform an under-the-eaves corner into a unified and functional bathing area. Decorative tile softens the look while allowing plenty of latitude for decorating schemes in the future.

UNDERSTATED PATTERNS

An abundance of contrast is not necessary to achieve a good design. Often one or two simple design elements are all that is required to give character and definition to a room. Here a subtle color pattern on the floor and some light detailing on the tub surround do the job. When a simple design is what you seek, try to establish a theme and carry it through the entire project.

In a tub that also contains a shower, plan to install tile from the top of the tub to about 6 inches above the showerhead. If the tub doesn't have a shower, tile at least 1 foot above the tub (more if you anticipate a lot of splashing). If you want to tile the ceiling as well, use a fast-setting adhesive; it will hold the tiles in place without support. (Install ceiling tile so that it doesn't have to line up with the wall tiles—say, diagonally—because getting it to fit will be very difficult.) If an end wall continues out past the tub, continue the tiles at least one full vertical row beyond the tub, and run the row down to the floor. Use bullnose cap tiles for the edges.

Set the tile on a backerboard substrate (see pages 130–131 for information on backerboard). The backerboard itself should be installed over a waterproofing membrane of 15-pound felt paper or 4-mil polyethylene. Overlay the edges of the membrane and seal the seams of the backerboard with fiberglass mesh tape bedded in adhesive.

If you have a window with wood casing and jambs, consider tearing it out or cutting back the casing and tiling the recess (see pages 56–57). You may want to eliminate the problems of a wood window altogether by installing glass blocks.

YOU'LL NEED

TIME: 2–3 days. A day to prepare the substrate, most of a day to tile, and a few hours to grout.

SKILLS: Cutting and installing backerboard, patching walls, cutting and installing tile.

TOOLS: Drill, hole saw, scraping tool, wall-patching tools, level, a straight board, notched trowel, snap cutter, nibbler, hacksaw with rod saw, grouting float.

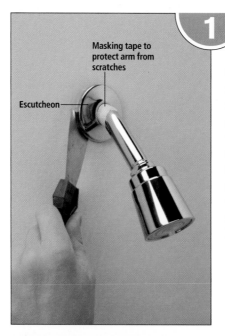

Masking tape to protect arm from scratches

Escutcheon

1 REMOVE THE HARDWARE.

Cutting and fitting tiles around fixtures is much easier if you first remove the hardware. Pry the shower-arm escutcheon away from the wall and perhaps remove the shower arm as well. Remove the tub spout; most can be unscrewed by sticking the handle of a screwdriver or hammer in the spout and turning counterclockwise. Remove the faucet handles and escutcheons.

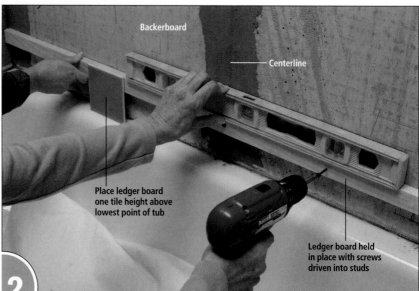

Backerboard

Centerline

Place ledger board one tile height above lowest point of tub

Ledger board held in place with screws driven into studs

2 PREPARE AND LAY OUT.

The walls must be solid and at least close to plumb and square (see page 123). If necessary, remove the existing substrate and install a waterproofing membrane and backerboard. Be sure the new surface is flush with any adjoining surface.

Establish a vertical reference line by laying the tiles in a row on the tub and making sure you will either have the same size tile on each end, or you will not have any very narrow pieces. If the end walls are out of square with the rear wall, factor in how the pieces will change size as you move upward. Establish a horizontal reference line, measuring from the low point of the tub if it is not level, and tack a very straight ledger board along its length.

3 CUT THE TILE.

Use a snap cutter for the straight cuts. Hold the tile in place and mark it for cutting. Align it on the cutter, score the surface by pushing down while sliding the cutter once across the tile, then push down on the handle. For a series of cuts the same size, use the adjustable guide. Smooth the ragged cut edges with a rubbing stone or file.

4 SET THE TILE.

Apply adhesive with a notched trowel, taking care not to cover your layout lines. Set the tiles, giving each a little twist and pushing to make sure it sticks. Start with the row sitting on the ledger. Most wall tiles are self-spacing. Once you have installed several rows and the adhesive has set, remove the ledger and install the bottom row.

5 CUT TILE AROUND PIPES.

Cuts around pipes usually do not have to be precise because the opening is covered with an escutcheon. Use a nibbler to eat away at a curved cut, or a hacksaw equipped with a rodsaw. To cut a hole, use a tile-cutting hole saw. Or set the tile on a piece of scrap wood, drill a series of closely spaced holes with a masonry bit, and tap out the hole.

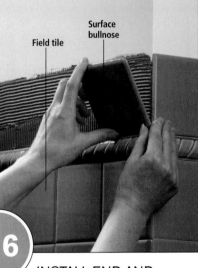

Field tile

Surface bullnose

6 INSTALL END AND CORNER TILES.

Cut the curved piece at the corner of the tub with a rod saw; it may take several attempts to get it just right. Use radius bullnose tiles everywhere there is an exposed edge. (Do not use a field tile edged with grout—it will look sloppy.)

Surface bullnose along top

7 TILE TO THE DESIRED HEIGHT.

When you reach your top row, wipe away excess adhesive from the wall as you install bullnose caps. Use outside corner pieces (down angles), which have two cap edges, at all outside corners.

Tiling a tub surround *(continued)*

8 ATTACH CERAMIC ACCESSORIES.

Apply adhesive and use masking tape to hold soap dishes and other accessories in place until they set. Take the tape off after a day or two and apply grout, but wait a week or so before using them.

9 GROUT, CAULK, AND SEAL.

Mix the grout with a latex additive and push it into the joints with a grouting float held nearly flat. Tip the float up and wipe away the excess. Carefully wipe the surface to produce consistent grout lines. Use a tool to shape the joints. Caulk the corners and edges. Wipe and dry-buff the tile until the haze is gone.

10 FASTEN THE HARDWARE.

Reattach the plumbing hardware. If you need to install a shower arm, use a thin tool handle to tighten it. If the new tile causes valves or nipples to be recessed too far and you can't install a faucet or spout, visit a plumbing supplier and pick up suitable extensions. Once the grout cures, apply sealer.

TILING AN ACCESS PANEL

Plumbing access panels are usually located in an adjoining room, but might be in the bathroom. The panel may have been installed when the bathroom was built, or it might have been built out of necessity when a plumber needed to gain access to the pipes and valves supplying the tub. Don't tile over the panel because a plumber may need to get in there again. The easiest solution is to cover the panel with a piece of plastic, well-painted plywood, or a plastic access panel made for the purpose (available at home centers). Or make a tiled access panel. Cut a piece of plywood sized to hold full tiles. Install tiles on it so they will align with the surrounding tiles, and trim the edges

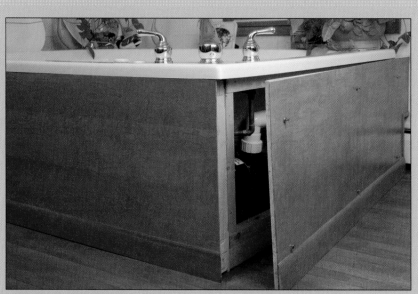

with painted wood molding; drive screws through the molding to hold the panel in place. Or skip the molding and attach with magnetic cabinet door catches.

TILING A SHOWER STALL

If you are building a new shower stall, the easiest approach is to install a prefabricated shower pan, and then tile above it. (A shower pan, or base, is the shower's floor, with a hole for the drain.) Several types of pans are available, and they are all fairly easy to install (see page 82). If you want the floor of the shower to be tiled as well, look for a pan that can be tiled over.

A 36-inch-square shower stall (the size is determined by the size of the pan) will be comfortable for an adult; a 32-inch stall will feel cramped. If a vented drain and water supply lines aren't in place, you will need to install them. Consult with or hire a plumber; it is especially important that the drain be properly vented.

Don't place the shower in a corner of the bathroom just to save work; framing new walls is a fairly small part of the job. Rather than tiling over existing walls that aren't plumb and square, start with plumb, square walls. It will be much easier to achieve a professional-looking tile job.

Use radius bullnose tiles where the edge of a tile will be visible, and corner pieces (down angles) where two edges will be visible. Decide exactly where you want the tiles to stop. For example you may want to wrap tile around the thickness of the walls where the shower door will be installed.

YOU'LL NEED

TIME: One day to install a shower pan and substrate, another day to tile, and a few hours to grout.

SKILLS: Framing walls, cutting and installing backerboard and tile, grouting.

TOOLS: Drill, hammer, chisel, circular saw, level, tiling and grouting tools.

1 BUILD THE ENCLOSURE.

Decide if you want to install a glass shower door or hang a curtain, and whether you want walls up to the ceiling. Build a 2×4 frame, plumb and square to adjoining walls, with blocking to support the plumbing.

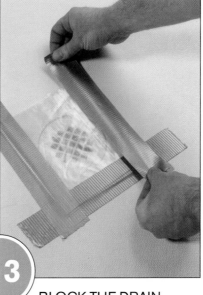

3 BLOCK THE DRAIN.

Before you begin preparing the substrate or tiling, tape a thick piece of plastic over the drain opening to keep out debris, which could clog the drain.

2 CHOOSE THE DRAIN.

The drain for most shower pans is a two-piece unit, usually made of cast iron or brass. Choose a drain that matches both your pan and the existing drain line. Ask your dealer to show you how to attach it to the pan and to the drain line.

4 REMOVE ANY OLD TILE.

If you need to remove old tile first, remove as much of the grout as possible surrounding the tiles, then use a hammer and a cold chisel to knock out the tiles. Wear eye protection and gloves.

Tiling a shower stall *(continued)*

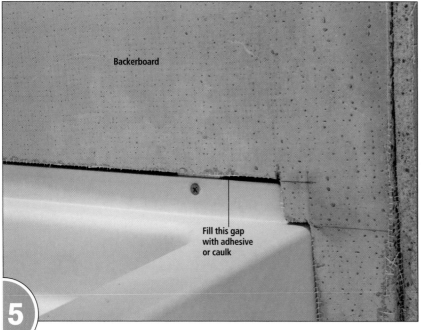

Backerboard

Fill this gap with adhesive or caulk

MAKING YOUR OWN TILED SHOWER PAN

If you want a tiled surface under your feet, you may be able to install tile directly onto a terrazzo pan. If you are adventurous, consider making your own pan—that way, it can be any dimension you like. Build the shower stall frame first, then lay a thick waterproofing membrane that will funnel water into the drain. Construct a pan substrate out of backerboard using mortar only—do not poke any holes in the membrane.

5 INSTALL THE PAN.

Set the pan in place, and check it for level in both directions; shim if necessary. Attach the drain to the pan and to the drain line, and test by pouring buckets of water down the drain. Most pans have a flange that fits tightly against the wall; you will install the backerboard slightly above the flange.

SHOWER PAN OPTIONS

Shower pans are fabricated out of fiberglass, acrylic, terrazzo, or other materials. These pans cannot be tiled. Buy the best quality you can afford. Thin, flimsy products will not last, because constant flexing in the pan can create leaks. Study the installation instructions of the pan before you buy it—sturdier, heavier models may require less framing.

In addition to a standard square shape, consider a larger pan with a seat or two, or a pentagonal shape (which typically is used with a three-sided glass door).

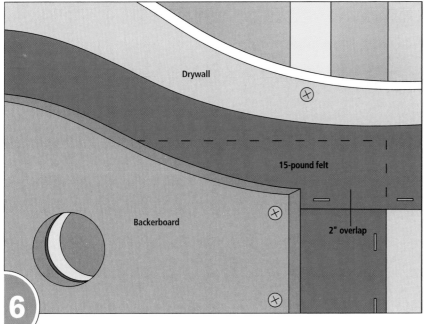

Drywall

15-pound felt

Backerboard

2" overlap

Plumb line

Level line

6 PREPARE THE SUBSTRATE.

Install the waterproofing membrane: Staple or nail 15-pound felt paper or 4-mil polyethylene to the studs (or drywall). Overlap upper sections of the membrane over the lower sections by at least 2 inches. Cut and install cement backerboard. Drill holes for the shower valves and spouts with a carbide-tipped hole saw. Attach with screws driven into studs. Keep the backerboard about ¼ inch above the shower pan, and fill the gap with silicone caulk or tile adhesive. Cover the joints with fiberglass mesh tape, and seal with tile adhesive.

7 LAY OUT THE TILES.

Carefully mark horizontal and vertical reference lines. Make sure you will not end up with small slivers of tiles in the corners, and avoid having different-size tiles on either side of a wall. Make sure your bullnose or trim tiles will fit properly along the edges.

8 SET THE TILES.

Apply tile adhesive with a notched trowel. Don't cover the reference lines. Use a batten board (see page 78). Give each tile a little twist as you push it into place. Wipe away any excess adhesive immediately. Allow the tiles to set at least a day before grouting.

9 INSTALL THE FINISH PLUMBING.

After the grout has dried, slide on the escutcheons and install the shower arm and head and the faucet handles. Make sure the area around the handle or handles is well sealed; if your unit does not have a rubber gasket that grabs tightly to the wall, apply a bead of silicone caulk.

10 INSTALL THE HARDWARE.

Mark hole locations to mount the door frame or curtainrod holders. Carefully drill through the tiles with a masonry bit. Apply silicone caulk to the back of the frame, and attach it by driving screws into a stud or into plastic anchors. Caulk the inside edges.

RENEWING A FIREPLACE WITH TILE

As houses are remodeled and updated, the style of the fireplace often gets overlooked. And after years of use a hearth and fireplace surround can become stained and damaged. Refacing a fireplace surround is not a difficult project, as long as the floor and wall are solid and in good repair. By investing a weekend and purchasing a small number of tiles, you can add a striking touch to your living room.

A beautified fireplace is not necessarily a safe fireplace, and a simple refacing cannot cure any internal problems. Have your fireplace and chimney inspected and cleaned before you begin.

EYE-CATCHING SOPHISTICATION
This eye-catching fireplace uses a sophisticated combination of tiles covering everything but the mantelpiece. Though not for beginners, it demonstrates the power of a few well-chosen decorative tiles.

TRADITIONAL SLATE
The use of stone tiles such as these handsome slates are a traditional choice for fireplace hearths and surrounds. In addition consider granite, marble, and brick veneer, and for hearths, flagstones.

NEUTRAL TONES
Use color and tile size to allow the fireplace to either blend in or stand apart from the room. The deep terra-cotta tones of these tiles are neutral enough to fit any color that future decorating styles may bring. The raised hearth puts the heat of the fireplace where it is the most beneficial; tile is the ideal surface for it.

TILING A FIREPLACE

Before beginning a remodeling project involving a fireplace, check your local building codes for requirements regarding the use of fire-resistant materials between the tile and a combustible wall. You may need to keep combustible materials, such as a mantelpiece, a specified distance from the firebox. The fireplace, damper, and chimney must be in good working condition, and the chimney should draw smoke out of the house easily. If the chimney has not been cleaned lately, have it inspected and cleaned before you begin setting tile.

If the existing surface around your fireplace is cracked or loose, consult with a professional before proceeding. Removing an old fireplace surround often entails disrupting the existing firebox and chimney, and that should not be done by an amateur.

CAUTION

HEAT-RESISTANT MATERIALS

The heat generated by a fireplace can destroy the bond of many adhesives. Organic mastics and some thinset mortars should not be used near a fireplace. Use only tiles and adhesives specifically made for heated surfaces.

YOU'LL NEED

TIME: About 1 day to install the tile, once the surface has been prepared.

SKILLS: Laying out, cutting, and installing floor and wall tile.

TOOLS: Notched trowel, rubber mallet, tile cutter, drill, hammer, grouting float, sponge.

DECORATIVE ELEMENTS.

The rich brown color of the decorative glazed listello and field tiles, framing this fireplace and hearth, add beauty and interest without taking away from the other design elements of the room, such as the windows, grand mirror, and tiled floor.

1 PREPARE THE SURFACE.

Treat the existing surface as you would any other substrate. Clean off all soot and dirt. Remove any high spots with a rubbing stone or sanding block. Vacuum thoroughly. If the surface is not flat enough for setting tiles, coat it with a thin coat of thinset mortar, and then create a level surface with latex-modified mortar (see page 39). Take care when laying out the installation around the fireplace opening. Here it would look especially sloppy to have cut tiles. Adjust the location of the tiles horizontally or vertically to minimize the need for cutting. If you have trouble with the layout, consider using smaller tiles.

Tiling a fireplace *(continued)*

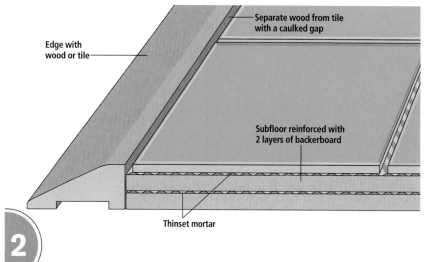

Edge with wood or tile

Separate wood from tile with a caulked gap

Subfloor reinforced with 2 layers of backerboard

Thinset mortar

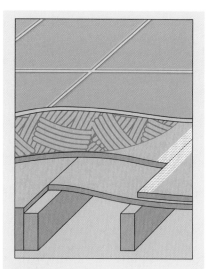

② TILE THE HEARTH.

If the hearth is surrounded by wood flooring, leave a gap around the perimeter the same width as the grout joints. Fill this gap with caulk or sealant once the tile has been grouted. The hearth is less affected by heat than the wall surround, but it must be strong enough to withstand firewood being dropped on it. If the existing hearth is less than 1⅛ inch thick, consider adding backerboard to strengthen the setting bed. If possible, use two layers of cement backerboard; bond them together and to the subfloor with thinset adhesive. Let the substrate cure for a couple of days, then set tiles.

EXTENDING A RAISED HEARTH.

To expand a raised hearth (found in some older homes), build a frame with 2×4s, plywood, and backerboard. Rip the 2×4s to the correct width, drill pilot holes, and screw them to the floor.

③ TILE THE SURROUND.

Because the surround is exposed to high temperatures, use only materials that are heat-resistant. The surround is frequently composed of a single row of large tiles around the opening, trimmed with molding on the sides and butting up against a mantel at the top. Consider trimming the surround with decorative tiles.

Attach a 1×2 batten across the top of the fireplace to support the top horizontal row of tiles. Leave the batten in place for about 24 hours, giving the adhesive time to set. If you are installing large, heavy tiles, you will have better luck building a larger support made out of three pieces of scrap lumber.

HEARTH MAINTENANCE

■ **Tile is not indestructible, and marble—which is often used for hearths—is easy to scratch and stain.** So don't abuse your hearth. Keep the grout well sealed to avoid stains from sooty wood. Buy and use a good grate or set of glass doors, to keep sparks contained. And don't use your fireplace unless it is drawing well, or you will get soot and smoke in your house.

■ **Many fireplace hearths are too small to offer adequate protection to the floor.** When installing new tile, go ahead and extend the substrate to add another course or two, so you won't have to worry about sparks singeing your wood floor or carpeting.

A wood stove radiates heat in all directions, so you must place it on a noncombustible surface and protect nearby walls. Follow local building codes and the manufacturer's recommendations to determine the best location for a stove, as well as the correct size of the noncombustible hearth and fire wall.

Use tile or, for a more traditional look, brick veneer. Also known as thin brick, brick veneer can be set much like tile, using thinset mortar. Or look for a ceramic tile that mimics the appearance of brick. Run the flue pipe before installing the tile.

SAFE INSTALLATION OF A WOOD-BURNING STOVE

Modern wood-burning stoves are highly efficient, burning logs completely and sending little heat up the chimney. Follow the manufacturer's installation instructions carefully. Use a masonry chimney or a class A metal flue. Be sure the chimney is high enough above the roof to draw well. Clean the flue regularly; burning wood produces creosote, which accumulates in the flue, creating a fire hazard.

YOU'LL NEED

TIME: 1 day to install the tile once the walls, chimney flue, and floor are prepared.

SKILLS: Laying out, cutting, and installing tile.

TOOLS: Hammer, tape measure, level, screwdriver, drill, tiling and grouting tools.

SIMPLE AND SAFE.

The size of the wood stove surround will depend on the size of the stove, manufacturer's recommendations, and local codes. This wood stove has a simple design that uses brick veneer to protect the floor and meet the basic safety considerations for the installation. If installing a wood stove for the first time, make sure your homeowners insurance covers it.

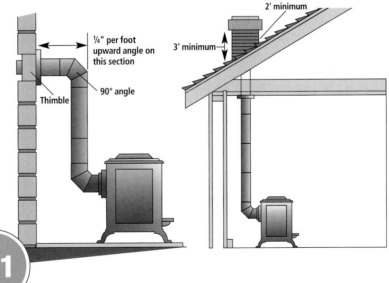

① PLAN THE LOCATION.

Shown above are two options for venting a wood-burning stove. You can install a masonry flue in the wall, or extend a class-A metal flue up through the roof. Before you begin the project, check local requirements for chimney height above the roof line. Assemble the chimney and flue first, so you know exactly where the stove needs to be located. As you assemble the metal chimney, fit the sections together with the male ends pointing toward the stove. That way any condensation and creosote will flow back toward the fire and dissipate.

Planning a wood stove surround *(continued)*

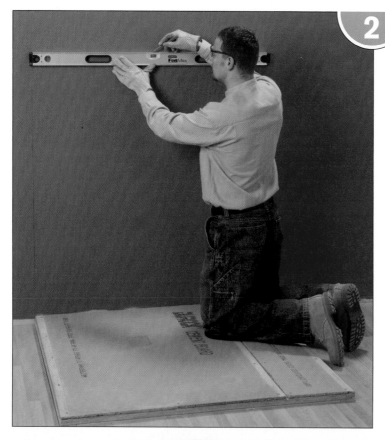

2 LAY OUT THE JOB.

Based on the manufacturer's recommendations and local codes, decide on the dimensions of your hearth and fire wall. Some stoves require that large floor and wall spaces be fire protected, while others have minimal requirements. You may want to cover large areas with tile because it looks attractive and is easy to clean. The dimensions shown on page 87 are typical for a medium-size wood stove.

Try to plan the layout so you can use full tiles for the entire installation. Take into account the width of the grout joints.

Cut away any carpeting and padding. Remove a section of baseboard molding wide enough to accommodate the fire wall. If required by code, first attach 1/4-inch-thick backerboard to the floor and wall. Screws on the wall should attach to studs.

3 SET THE TILE.

Dry-fit the tiles for the hearth and the first row on the wall. Move the hearth tiles out of the way. Mix thinset mortar with liquid latex. When applying the tile to the wall, check for level and plumb with a carpenter's level. Use plastic spacers to maintain consistent joints between the tiles.

To set the hearth tiles, start in a corner and lay the row that meets the wall first, taking care to line up the hearth grout joints with the wall grout joints. If necessary use a snap cutter to cut tiles. Wait a day for the tile adhesive to set, then grout the joints.

TAKING TILE OUTDOORS

Tile can be a wonderful material for exterior patios, porches, pool surrounds, and walkways. In mild climates tile has been used for thousands of years. In cold climates, however, tile has been used sparingly—and often unsuccessfully—outdoors. That is largely because the freeze-thaw cycle causes the ground to expand and contract beyond what a tile installation can endure.

Today that concern has lessened. New materials and installation techniques now allow tile to be used in cold climates with much greater success. Select tiles for patios, porches, and walkways that have a nonslip surface. Vitreous and impervious tiles absorb the least amount of water, making them better able to withstand freezing weather. In regions with a varied climate, all of the setting materials must be labeled as freeze/thaw stable for installations in cold climates.

CLIMATE SENSITIVE
Unglazed pavers cut the glare in sunny locations and are an easy-to-maintain choice for outdoor living spaces, particularly in warm climates. Because of their water absorption, they can't withstand the freeze/thaw cycle of colder climates.

SMOOTH BOUNDARIES
In addition to giving you a chance to add color and style to a pool, tile is less abrasive than concrete or brick, and so makes an ideal edging material for pools. Using it as a decorative feature in combination with brick and concrete keeps costs down. Installing tile in outdoor food preparation areas and patios are good projects for do-it-yourselfers, but tiling a pool is a job for professionals.

Taking tile outdoors *(continued)*

MEDITERRANEAN STYLE
This wall fountain pops with color and gives a warm and sunny feel with blue and yellow Mediterranean ceramic tiles and a sun fixture. Sealed terra-cotta tiles act as a grounding border.

OUTDOOR ENTERTAINMENT
Naturally heat-resistant stone tiles give this outdoor kitchen the practical utility to stand up to cooking needs and the elements. See page 103 for step-by-step instructions on tiling an outdoor countertop.

VISUAL ACCENTS

The small blue accent tiles add visual interest to a seemingly regular tiled patio. In a warm climate, as is apparent in the featured patio, almost any floor-rated tile will work. See page 96-98 for instructions on laying patio tile.

ITALIAN INTRICACY

The Italian glass mosaic tiles used in this pool installation echo the calming feel of the color and sound of the pool water. A project of this scope however, is not the job for a do-it-yourselfer. Enlist the help of a professional.

LAYING A CONCRETE PATIO SUBSTRATE

An outdoor tile surface in most places needs to rest on a solid substrate of concrete. Installing a new concrete slab is a major undertaking. Talk with your local building inspector and find out the requirements for your area; these regulations are there to ensure that a slab will survive in your climate. In areas with severe winters, it is important to lay a well-tamped bed of gravel before pouring the concrete, so water can drain away before it has a chance to freeze and crack your concrete surface.

Here we show you how to install a surface that is smooth enough to receive tile. If the prospect of building forms and pouring concrete is daunting, hire a contractor to handle that part of the job for you. Do not tile over an existing concrete patio without first examining it, then preparing it (see page 95).

1 EXCAVATE THE SITE.

Use mason's line and stakes to mark the perimeter and height of the new slab. Allow for the slab to slope down away from the house ¼ inch for every running foot. Remove the sod and topsoil to reach the desired depth. If you want to use the sod elsewhere, undercut it horizontally about 2 inches beneath the surface and cut it into easy-to-handle sections. Save enough to resod around the edges of the new slab. If you plan to place gravel or sand beneath the slab, excavate at least 5 inches deeper. Check the depth from time to time as you dig. Lay a straight 2×4 on edge on the dirt; measure from its top edge (3½ inches) to the mason's line.

YOU'LL NEED

TIME: 2–3 days. With two helpers, 1 day to excavate, ½ day to build forms, and 1 day to pour and finish the concrete.

SKILLS: Measuring and cutting wood, checking for square, driving stakes, fastening with nails or screws, screeding, finishing concrete (a special skill—have an experienced finisher at least give you advice.

TOOLS: Hammer, circular saw, carpenter's level, shovels, wheelbarrows, rake, screed, bull float or darby, broom, concrete finishing trowels.

2 INSTALL THE FORMS.

Use straight 2×4s or 2×6s for the forms (depending on the desired slab thickness). Anchor the forms by driving 2×4 stakes, and pounding two double-headed nails through the stakes and into the form. Place your foot against the opposite side of the forms to make nailing easier. Be sure the tops of the forms are level with or above the tops of the stakes. Support each board with 18-inch-long stakes every 3 to 4 feet. Make sure the forms are square and properly sloped away from the house.

DIVIDE A LARGE SLAB.

Roll reinforcing mesh out, and cut it to fit. Adding dividers on a large patio allows you to pour and finish manageable amounts of concrete. If the dividers will be temporary, use any straight length of lumber. If you plan to leave the divider in as part of the slab, use pressure-treated lumber or redwood. At right, two 2×2s sandwich the mesh, keeping it at the right height for maximum effectiveness.

INSTALL PERMANENT DIVIDERS.

Install permanent dividers every 12 feet. Brush on a coat of wood sealer to enhance rot resistance. Put masking tape on the top edges to keep wet concrete from staining the wood and to avoid scratching the forms when you screed. Drive interior stakes 1 inch below the top of the permanent dividers so they will not be visible once the concrete is poured.

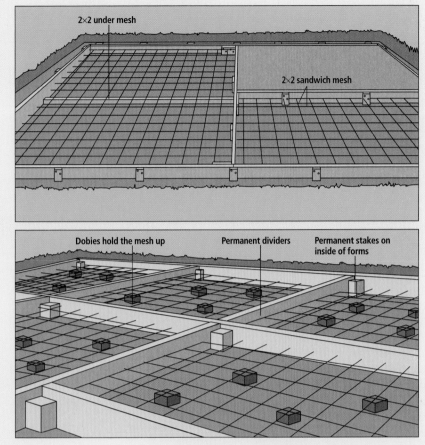

2×2 under mesh

2×2 sandwich mesh

Dobies hold the mesh up   Permanent dividers   Permanent stakes on inside of forms

3 TRANSPORT THE CONCRETE ON RAMPS.

Mix your concrete as near to the site as possible; do not use curing compounds. Or have the ready-mix truck park as close as is safe. (A concrete truck weighs enough to crack sidewalks and driveways.) Wet concrete is heavy: Keep wheelbarrow loads small enough to handle. To cross soft soil or lawns, lay a walkway of 2×10 or 2×12 planks. Build ramps over the forms so you do not disturb them. Use two or more wheelbarrows to keep the job moving.

4 DUMP AND MOVE THE CONCRETE.

Start dumping concrete in the farthest corner of the forms. Dump it in mounds that reach ½ inch or so above the top of the form. It helps to have one person working a shovel while others run the wheelbarrows. The shoveler directs the wheelbarrow handlers and tells them where to dump the concrete. Wear gloves and heavy boots that fit snugly. Pace your efforts because you'll be moving a lot of concrete before the pour is completed.

Laying a concrete patio substrate *(continued)*

5 PULL UP
REINFORCING MESH.

While pouring the concrete, use a hoe, rake, or shovel to pull the wire mesh up into the concrete. For the greatest strength, keep the mesh positioned halfway between the bottom of the excavation and the finished surface of the slab. Watch that the mesh doesn't get pushed against the form at any point. Keep it 1 to 2 inches away from all forms.

6 TAMP CONCRETE TO
REMOVE AIR POCKETS.

For best results, the concrete should flow completely to the forms and dividers and contain no air pockets. Run a shovel up and down along the inside edge of all the forms and tap the sides of the forms with a hammer. Be sure to check that all corners are filled in and tamped adequately.

7 SCREED WITH A
STRAIGHTEDGE.

Begin screeding (also called leveling) as soon as you've filled the first 3 or 4 feet of the length of the form. Keep both ends of the screed—a straight 2×4—pressed down on the top of the form while moving it back and forth in a sawing motion and drawing it toward the unleveled concrete. If depressions occur, fill them in with concrete and screed again.

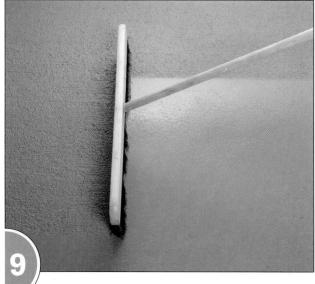

8 FLOAT THE SURFACE.

Screed a second time, to make sure the surface is level with the forms. To smooth the surface, run a bull float in long, back-and-forth motions, slightly raising its leading edge so it does not dig into the concrete. If you use a hand-held float, called a darby, work in large, sweeping arcs.

9 BROOM THE FINISH.

For a smooth finish, professionals use a steel trowel. For a tiling project, a broom finish is fine. Dampen the broom and pull it—do not push it. Have a brick or piece of 2×4 handy so you can knock the broom now and again to keep it clean.

PREPARING A CONCRETE SURFACE

You can tile over an existing concrete patio that's in good condition as long as it is at least 3 inches thick, sloped to allow water to drain off, and free from serious cracks. If the patio has a crack that keeps growing every year, or if one side of the crack is higher than the other, then it has structural problems. Don't tile over a slab in such a condition. Also ensure that the slab is sitting slightly above ground level and is cleaned of any oil, dirt, or curing compounds.

YOU'LL NEED

TIME: 1 hour for most patches.

SKILLS: Spreading patching compound smoothly.

TOOLS: Concrete trowel, mason's trowel, 2×4, grinding tool, hose, stiff brush.

PATCH CRACKS.

Fill small cracks or other irregularities with a concrete patching compound. Latex and epoxy compounds work well. Or use sand-mix concrete mixed with a latex additive.

FILL IN LOW SPOTS.

Use a straightedge to locate low spots on a patio. Screed a patching or self-leveling compound over the low spots to create a flat surface. Finish with a trowel and/or broom to match the surrounding surface.

REPAIR EDGES.

If concrete is broken along the edges of the patio, chip away any loose concrete, then clean and wet the area. Place a board along the damaged area, then fill with patching compound or fresh mortar. Smooth with a trowel and allow to set.

ROUGHEN THE SURFACE.

If the patio has a smooth, steel-troweled finish, you may have to roughen the surface before tiling. Use a grinding tool with an abrasive wheel. A tool rental store may have a floor sander designed for concrete slabs.

CLEAN THE SURFACE.

Scrub the surface with water and a stiff brush. Use a degreaser to remove oil and grease stains. If the patio is smooth and dirty, rent a power washer with at least 4,000 psi to clean and roughen the surface simultaneously.

LAYING PATIO TILE

An outdoor tile surface comes under a good deal of stress, so use the best-quality materials available for each step. Talk with your tile dealer about specific products that will perform best outdoors. Don't give water any chance to enter or hide beneath your tiled surface. Pack the grout joints as tightly as possible, then seal them carefully. Renew the grout sealer, and caulk or seal in expansion joints regularly.

YOU'LL NEED

TIME: 1–2 days. About 1 day to install 100 square feet of tile; 1–2 hours a day or two later to grout it.

SKILLS: Cutting and installing tile.

TOOLS: Notched trowel, snap cutter or wet saw, rubber mallet and beater block, grouting float, level, sponge.

1 APPLY AN ISOLATION MEMBRANE.

A trowel-applied isolation membrane is a caulk-like substance that never fully hardens. It forms a layer that separates the tile from the patio, making it less likely that cracks in the concrete will translate to the grout and tile. Apply it with the notched side of the trowel, then smooth it with the flat side.

2 DRY-SET THE TILES.

Allow the isolation membrane to cure. Lay the tiles in a dry run over at least part of the surface before mixing any adhesive; this is particularly important if you will be setting tiles in a pattern. If the patio is slightly out-of-square, dry-setting gives you a chance to judge how best to arrange and cut tiles.

3 USE A WET SAW.

For thick tile or stone, or to cut inside corners accurately, rent a wet saw. It quickly and cleanly slices through the hardest of materials, even granite. To keep the blade from eroding too quickly, keep water running on it at all times.

4 APPLY THE MORTAR.

Use thinset mortar mixed with a liquid latex additive. Apply the mortar in two steps. Trowel on a smooth base coat about ½-inch thick. Then comb the surface with the notched side of the trowel. Use long, sweeping strokes.

5 SET THE TILE.

Give each tile a twist as you push it into the adhesive. Take care not to slide the tile into position. Use spacers to keep the tiles aligned. If the tiles are not flush, use a beater block and hammer or a rubber mallet to gently tap them into alignment.

6

ENSURE THE SURFACE IS LEVEL.

Prior to grouting the joints, you can ensure that your tile surface is horizontally level by using a level and straight board. A level surface will allow you to smoothly move the grouting float across the tiles, making sure to get each joint fully packed with grout. Place the level on top of a straight board that is longer than the level itself. This will prevent the level from dipping into a crack and will allow you to measure a larger radius. If you find there is a great discrepancy in the tile, you can use a beater block and a rubber mallet to gently even out the tile surface.

APPLY SEALANT.

Applying sealant to outdoor tiles and grout is essential to help prevent water from seeping beneath the tile surface. Take special care to select a sealant that is specific to outdoor use. You can apply sealant once the grout has cured. (It is recommended to wait two weeks.) Make sure that you are working with a clean, dry surface. First, using a sponge mop, apply a coat of sealant to the tiles. Let dry. Second, wearing protective gloves, use a small sponge to apply the sealant directly onto the grout. You will want to reapply tile and grout sealant about once every six months to keep your outdoor tiles protected.

7

GROUT THE JOINTS.

Allow time for the adhesive to cure (usually one or two days). Mix the grout of your choice, using latex additive to keep it from cracking later on. Push the grout into the joints with a grouting float, making sure you move the float in at least two directions at all points. When the joints in a small section are fully packed, scrape with the float held nearly perpendicular to the tiles to remove as much waste as possible. Clean the grout from the tile surface and after the surface has dried, buff with a dry towel. Lastly, clean the expansion joints of any leftover adhesive and run a neat bead of caulk along the joints. Shape the joints, if you like, with the backside of a spoon, a dampened rag, or your finger.

8

EXPANSION JOINTS

Tile is going to expand and contract on a patio installation even more than it will indoors. You can minimize damage due to this movement by placing expansion joints between tiles no more than 16 feet apart and wherever the tile meets another surface, such as the foundation of the house or stairs. Ideally an expansion joint should fall over a similar joint in the concrete pad. After grouting the other joints, fill the expansion joints with caulk or sealant.

MINIMIZE CRACKING

Grout. A gentle breeze on a sunny day may be refreshing, but it may have an adverse impact on the grout drying process. Minimize cracks that develop as a result of a too-fast drying process. Cover the patio with a polyethylene tarp. Use a garden hose with a spray attachment to mist the surface of the tarp, allowing the grout to dry slowly.

Concrete. Concrete may appear solid, but it is really quite porous. Concrete readily absorbs moisture. Hose down the slab surface prior to applying thinset. This will reduce the tendency of concrete to draw moisture out of the thinset, causing it to dry too quickly and crack.

Laying patio tile *(continued)*

DEFINE A DINING AREA
The tile on this outdoor patio defines the dining area and gives it a more formal appearance than the brick used on the surrounding patio.

HEARTH MAINTENANCE

■ **Tile is not indestructible, and marble–which is often used for hearths–is easy to scratch and stain.** So don't abuse your hearth. Keep the grout well sealed to avoid stains from sooty wood. Buy and use a good grate or set of glass doors, to keep sparks contained. And don't use your fireplace unless it is drawing well, or you will get soot and smoke in your house.

■ **Many fireplace hearths are too small to offer adequate protection to the floor.** When installing new tile, go ahead and extend the substrate to add another course or two, so you won't have to worry about sparks singeing your wood floor or carpeting.

GLAZED TILE

You may be tempted to use glazed tiles for your outdoor patio floor, but you should reconsider. Glazed tiles become very slippery when wet. It is best to reserve glazed tiles for vertical surfaces or raised planters. The bold colors and vibrant designs currently available in glazed tiles will make a great decorative accent.

TILING OUTDOOR STEPS

Although rare in new construction, tiled stairs have a long and rich history. You can add tile to both the risers and the treads of a concrete stairway. On a wood stairway, a popular choice is to install tiles on the risers only. Risers are not stepped on, so they can be covered with thin wall tiles if you prefer. Cover the entire riser, or use a few decorative tiles as accents. Large, unglazed paver or quarry tiles are attractive for exterior treads. The tiles should be at least ½-inch thick and slip resistant. Special bullnose tiles are available that can extend over the riser. Install riser tiles before you install the tread tiles.

PREPARING CONCRETE STAIRS.

Concrete stairs are the best surface for tile. But the concrete must be in solid condition, with no major cracks or other structural damage. Seal small cracks with a concrete-patching compound. Repair damaged edges by chipping away any loose concrete, then sweeping and wetting the area. Place a board along the damaged area, then fill it with patching compound or fresh mortar. Smooth with a trowel and allow to set.

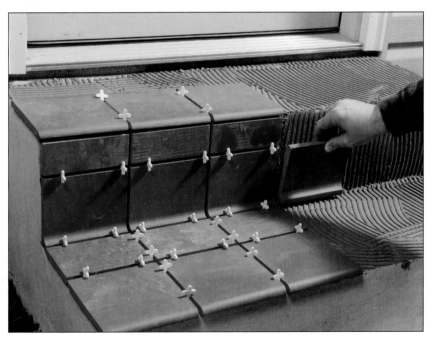

TILING CONCRETE STAIRS.

The most professional installation calls for a new mortar setting bed applied over the entire surface. But you can also tile over concrete stairs following the general guidelines for a concrete patio (see pages 95–97).

Remove oily stains and make sure the concrete surface does not contain curing compounds. Spread a trowel-applied isolation membrane before setting tiles. Use bullnose and cove tiles, as shown, to strengthen the edges and make cleanup easier.

Tiling outdoor steps *(continued)*

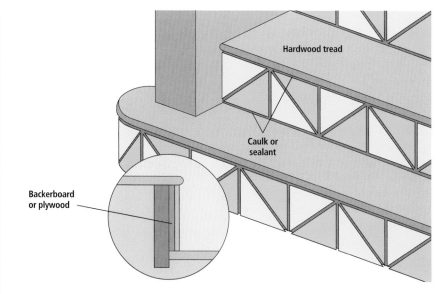

TILING THE RISERS ONLY.

Combine tiled risers with hardwood treads for an appealing contrast. Use standard wall tiles or natural stone tiles. If possible, install plywood or backerboard for a smooth substrate. Set the tiles in adhesive, and seal the top and bottom edges with caulk or sealant rather than grout.

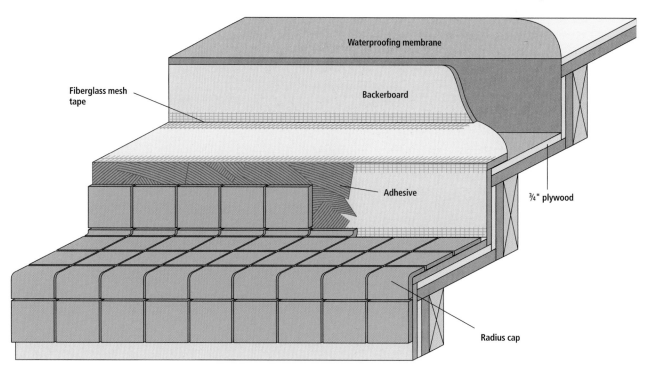

TILING OVER WOOD STAIRS.

Take special care here to ensure that the substrate will not flex when walked on. The stair frame must be solid, inflexible, and in good condition. Cover the treads, risers, and any landings with exterior-grade ¾-inch plywood. Then lay waterproofing membrane over the whole job. Install backerboard over the membrane. Use only tiles and setting materials suitable for exterior installations. Use bullnose caps wherever a tile edge is exposed. If you are planning to tile over an existing stair, you may have to adjust the heights of the landings at the top and bottom to keep the stairs safe and up to code.

TILING A GARDEN BENCH

A garden can be a great extension of your living space, creating the utility of an extra room for relaxing or entertaining. One way to tie in the tiling you've incorporated indoors or to accent your tile outdoors is by tiling accessories—for example, a garden bench. This project can be fairly inexpensive if you already have the bench. As with your other outside projects, if you live in a warm climate, almost any tile will work; however, in a climate where temperatures fall below freezing, don't use nonvitreous tile. Select an exterior-grade tile that is freeze thaw resistant. If you don't want to worry about selecting weather-appropriate tiles, consider bringing the outside in for the winter. Brighten up an entryway, a screened-in porch, or playroom with the garden bench. When choosing and setting tiles, keep in mind that you want the bench to be comfortable to sit on; therefore, you don't want the tiles to be raised. Use bullnose tiles on the edges.

YOU'LL NEED

TIME: 2–3 days. 1 day to lay the tile, 24 hours to cure, 1 day to grout. You will seal the tiles 2 weeks later.

SKILLS: Dry-setting tile, setting tiles, grouting and sealing tiles.

TOOLS: Pencil, straightedge, level, rubber mallet and beater block, notched trowel, grouting and sealing tools.

INDOOR/OUTDOOR IRON

A tiled wrought-iron bench or table also makes a very attractive piece that can easily be brought indoors during the winter months. See pages 105–107 for tiling a bistro table.

1 DRY-SET THE TILES.

First find the center of the bench. You can do this by drawing diagonal lines between opposite corners. Once you have your center point, lay out your center tiles and work out to the edges, setting your field tiles next. If you have any cut tiles, keep them symmetrical at the front and the back of the bench, or perhaps all the way around the bench, acting as a border. Place the cut edges facing inward. By measuring the bench ahead of time, you may be able to select tiles that will fit the dimensions exactly.

Tiling a garden bench *(continued)*

2 MARK LOCATIONS FOR TILES.

During dry-setting, mark the specific locations on the bench for the tiles using a pencil and a straightedge. If necessary use a wet saw to cut tiles, being careful to lay out and mark any cut tiles on the border or the back of the bench.

3 APPLY THINSET.

Using a notched trowel, apply latex-modified thinset mortar to the center tiles. The notches help create uniform mortar thickness. By working in small sections, you don't have to worry about the thinset mortar drying before you can set the tiles.

4 SET CENTER TILES.

Press the center tiles firmly into the thinset. Use spacers to help preserve straight lines. Use a rubber mallet and beater block to gently tap the tiles into place.

5 SET FIELD AND BORDER TILES.

Once the center tiles are set, continue setting the field tiles. While you're setting the tiles, use a beater block and mallet to ensure they are being set evenly. Check with a straightedge or level.

6 APPLY GROUT AND SEALER.

Apply a sanded epoxy grout, taking special care to spread it into the joints until they are filled almost flush with the surface. Let the grout set, and then use a wet sponge to clean. See page 149 for more information on cleaning tiles. In about 2 weeks, once the grout has cured, apply an outdoor sealer to protect against the elements.

BROKEN TILE ALTERNATIVE

Consider using broken tiles for a more whimsical creation. You can create intricate designs with broken tiles or you can simply create free-form designs. For more information on working with broken tiles see page 107. When breaking and working with broken tiles always use your protective gloves and eyewear.

TILING AN OUTDOOR COUNTERTOP

This project shows you how to spice up an outdoor cooking center by adding tile to the countertop. Begin with a cooking center that has a concrete-tiled backerboard substrate. When selecting tile and tile treatments, remember to consider your climate. In warm climates almost any tile will work; in cold climates don't use glazed or nonvitreous tile. For grouting, use a more durable grout that will stand up to outdoor conditions. Consider using heat-resistant stone on the countertop that can easily handle hot pots and pans, and save your creativity and ceramic tiles for the backsplash.

A SOLID FOUNDATION.

Before you start tiling your outdoor cooking center, you want to make sure you have a solid base, including a concrete tiled backerboard subsurface. Also, confirm that you have all of the materials and tools on hand that you will need in order to complete the project, taking special care that the materials are conducive for the outdoors in your climate.

YOU'LL NEED

TIME: 3–4 days (not including the building of the cabinet and subsurface). 1-2 days to set the tiles, 24 hours to cure, and 1 day to apply finished touches.

SKILLS: Dry-setting tile, tiling a countertop, using a wet saw.

TOOLS: Wet saw, spacers, notched trowel, masking tape, screws, cleaning, grouting and sealing tools.

1 DRY-SETTING THE TILE.

Lay out the tiles on the substrate, using spacers for the grout lines. If you start the layout at the grill top, you can make sure you have the tiles symmetrical on either side of the grill. Now is the time to make adjustments to your design, before you apply the thinset mortar. You want to avoid slivers of cut tiles. If you are going to have a row of smaller-size tiles, place them at the back of the countertop.

Tiling an outdoor countertop *(continued)*

2 CUT THE TILES.

After the dry run, use a wet saw to cut the tiles to size. Keep in mind the size of the grout lines.

3 SET THE TILES.

Set the field tiles first, using spacers to keep grout lines even. When installing the backsplash, keep about ⅛-inch, or the size of a grout line, above the countertop tiles. Later you will apply caulk along this joint.

4 ATTACH THE EDGE TILES.

Back-butter the tiles and apply them to the edge. You can use masking tape to hold the tiles in place while the thinset mortar hardens or, as an alternative method, you can drive screws under the tiles. Check the tiles often to make sure they are not shifting down.

5 APPLY FINISHING TOUCHES.

Apply the sanded epoxy grout, taking special care to spread the grout into the joints until they are flush with the surface. Once the grout has hardened, use a damp sponge to clean the tiles. Apply caulk to the joint between the backsplash and the countertop. In about 2 weeks, seal the grout with a silicone sealant to prevent moisture from seeping behind the tiles.

TILING A BISTRO TABLE

A tiled bistro table can really liven up a patio, but it can be a time- and detail-intensive project. If you already have the bistro table, it will help cut down on the cost of the project. If you want to create a specific design, it is important to carefully plan your design before you begin the project. Drawing out the design with colored pencils on graph paper will help you determine any design flaws and will save you a lot of time in the end. Keep in mind your climate and other outdoor tile projects when selecting the tile and space for your bistro table. If the table is going to be outdoors, you want to use an sanded epoxy grout that is more durable, and will stand up to the elements. Grout is not waterproof, however, so let it set for 2 weeks, then apply a grout sealer.

TABLE FOR TWO.

A tiled bistro table, as pictured here, it can bring life to an enclosed porch or sunroom, even in the middle of winter. It's perfect as a decorative element, or as the ideal spot to share your morning cup of coffee with a friend or family member. And it's a great introductory do-it-yourself project—read on for step-by-step instructions.

YOU'LL NEED

TIME: 3–5 days. 1 day to plan the design. 1 day to set the tiles. 24 hours to cure. 1 day to grout. A sealer will be applied 2 weeks later.

SKILLS: Dry-setting tile, mosaic tiling, grouting techniques.

TOOLS: Colored pencils, graph paper, masking tape, notched trowel, spacers, tiling and grouting tools.

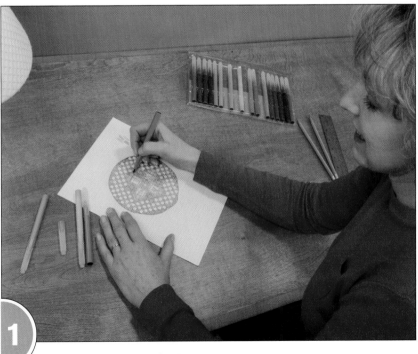

1 **DESIGN THE LAYOUT.**

Plan the design of your bistro table before you start laying and setting the tiles. Use colored pencils and graph paper. This allows you to experiment with more than one idea and will help you create a successful design.

Tiling a bistro table *(continued)*

2 SET THE TRIM TILES.

Back-butter the edge or trim tiles (or V-cap) with a thinset mortar and set. You can use masking tape to hold the tiles in place while the thinset mortar hardens. Check the tiles often to make sure they are not shifting down.

3 DRY-SET THE TILES.

To find the center of the tabletop, draw diagonal lines across the diameter. Once you have the center point, dry-fit the center tiles using spacers for the grout lines and work outward from there. If you have any cut tiles, keep them symmetrical around the edge of the tabletop. Adjust the center tiles and make any necessary cuts.

4 APPLY THINSET MORTAR.

Using a notched trowel, apply the thinset mortar to a small section of the tabletop. Make sure you can set the tiles before the adhesive sets up. Set the tile using spacers.

5 ADD FINISHING TOUCHES.

Apply the sanded epoxy grout, taking special care to spread the grout even with the tiles. Once the grout has hardened, use a damp sponge to clean the tiles. In about 2 weeks, seal the grout with a silicone sealant to prevent moisture from seeping behind the tiles.

SETTING BROKEN TILES

For a twist on tiling a bistro table (pages 105–106), craft a table with leftover broken tiles from other tiling projects. This is a great beginner's project as it does not require precision. You can be methodical in planning the design, or you can be whimsical and lay out the tiles free-form, letting the design emerge. Remember, if the table is going to be outdoors, you must use a grout and sealant that will endure all weather conditions. (see pages 117 and 119).

YOU'LL NEED

TIME: 3–5 days. 1 day to break up tiles and plan design. 1 day to set tiles. 24 hours to cure. 1 day to grout. Apply sealer 2 weeks later.

SKILLS: Dry-setting tiles, mosaic tiling, grouting.

TOOLS: Hammer, self-sealing plastic bag, rubber mallet, beater block, tile nippers, protective gloves and eyewear.

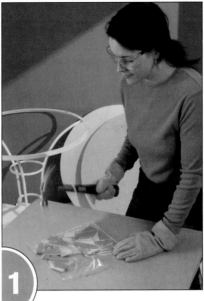

1 BREAK UP THE TILES.

Place your broken tiles in a self-sealing bag or wrap them in a towel. Use a hammer to break them down into smaller mosaic-size tiles. If a cleaner look is desired, you can give a straight-line cut to the tiles using tile nippers.

2 CUT PLYWOOD AND ATTACH BACKERBOARD.

Cut a sheet of thin water-resistant exterior-grade plywood the same size as the tabletop. Attach a piece of cement backerboard to the plywood.

3 DRY-SET THE TILES.

Arrange the tiles into the desired pattern, keeping the size of the grout lines consistent. If you are adding specific features to the pattern, such as spelling out a name or adding a moon or stars, you may want to draw them on the backerboard.

4 SET THE TILES.

With a notched trowel, mix and apply thinset mortar to a small section of the backerboard. Set the tiles into the thinset mortar. Repeat until the tabletop is complete. Use a beater block to level the tiles.

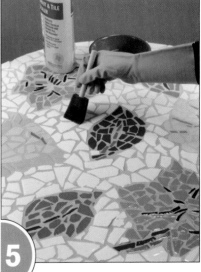

5 GROUT AND SEAL.

Allow the thinset mortar to cure for 24 hours. Apply a sanded grout. Apply the grout level with the overall height of the tiles for a smooth surface. Once the grout has cured (wait 2 weeks), apply an outdoor grout sealer for protection from the elements.

Tools
AND MATERIALS

Acquiring a basic knowledge of the tools and materials needed to successfully plan and complete a tiling project will prove beneficial during the planning and execution phases of your project. If you're following a project budget, be sure to account for the cost of tools. If you've done your research, you won't be running out to pick up a forgotten tool in the middle of the project. Some of the tools will already be in your toolbox at home, but there are others that you will either need to purchase or rent. If you think you'll be using the tool often, go ahead and purchase it, but if you think this is a one-time use, you're probably better off renting. Look in the phone book for tool rental shops in your area. Another great resource is your tile supplier, who may have the tools available for rent.

When purchasing tools, keep in mind that a better quality tool will last longer and perform better than an expensive one. You don't necessarily need the top-of-the-line, but you probably don't want the bottom-of-the-line either. You may want to rent power tools, such as the wet saw or a diamond-tipped cutter.

Once you have the tools, be sure to use them properly. The following pages provide information on the tools needed for laying out, cutting, and installing tile, and in some cases, instructions on how to use them. You will learn how to cut with a circular saw and read tips on drilling holes in ceramic tile. In addition you'll find guidelines for selecting grout, caulks, and sealers—using the proper material for these finishing touches is crucial to the success of your tiling project.

GROUT CONTRAST

This elegant black-and-white bathroom incorporates the beauty of stone and ceramic tile. Various shades of gray cut tiles are used to break up the wall tile, adding beauty and interest. Grout can play an integral part in your design—notice the use of different colored grout to create contrast. See page 113 for choosing grouting tools.

BROKEN BEAUTY

This ornate, broken mosaic bistro table is the perfect finishing touch to this brightly designed space. While a free-form mosaic would be an easier project for a beginner, with the right tools this can be a great project for a do-it-yourselfer. You'll need the bistro table and broken tiles, as well as protective eyewear and gloves. See page 107 to learn how to tile a bistro table with broken tiles.

CAREFUL PLANNING

This bathroom displays a beautifully executed design—mixing different types of tile, shape, and color. A combination of natural stone, glass mosaic tile and glazed ceramic tile create this unique design. This type of layout requires careful planning—drawing out your design on graph paper beforehand is recommended. See page 110 for selecting layout tools.

CUT SAVVY

When adding detail to a design, you will often need to cut tiles. The type of tile cutter you use will depend on the type of tile and the size of your project. A snap cutter would be appropriate for the design pictured here. See page 111 for details on choosing cutting tools.

SELECTING LAYOUT TOOLS

Layout involves measuring, marking, and determining the placement of tiles. The tools required are inexpensive hand tools. You may own most of them already.

For making scale drawings, graph paper is often the best material to use. You can buy graph paper with various sizes of grids; ¼-inch is the most common. For larger projects, measure the area to be tiled and sketch it so each ¼-inch grid square represents 1 square foot. For smaller projects, use a scale of 1 inch equals 1 foot. The only accessories you will need are a ruler, pencil, and eraser. Graph paper also comes in handy when sketching tile designs; just let each grid represent a tile.

An engineer's rule can be used in place of graph paper. An engineer's rule has three sides, with different scales marked along each edge. It allows you to quickly convert measured distances to scale, or to count the grids on graph paper. The trick is to choose a scale that will fit on the paper.

A combination square or a framing square can be used for measuring short distances and precisely marking square corners. You can get by with one or the other, but chances are that you will use both of them if they are available. A framing square also can double as a straightedge to aid in layout and tile installation. Or you can use short, straight boards, called layout sticks (see right).

A tape measure is indispensible for laying out and marking tiles for cutting. You also must have an accurate 2- or 4-foot level to check horizontal and vertical surfaces for plumb and to mark accurate layout lines.

An inexpensive plumb bob is necessary for finding plumb, and a chalk line allows you to quickly mark layout lines. Most chalk lines perform double duty as plumb bobs. Buy yellow chalk for dark tile and blue chalk for light-colored tile so you'll be able to clearly see your mark.

MAKE A LAYOUT STICK.

When tiling large, flat surfaces, one of the handiest tools is one you can make yourself. A layout stick is just a homemade ruler that allows you to lay out an installation without having to measure and mark for each tile location. Line up a row of tiles on a flat surface, with spacers between. Set a straight piece of pine alongside the tiles. Start at one end of the stick and mark the width of the grout joint between each tile. You will need a new layout stick if you change tiles or grout widths on a new installation.

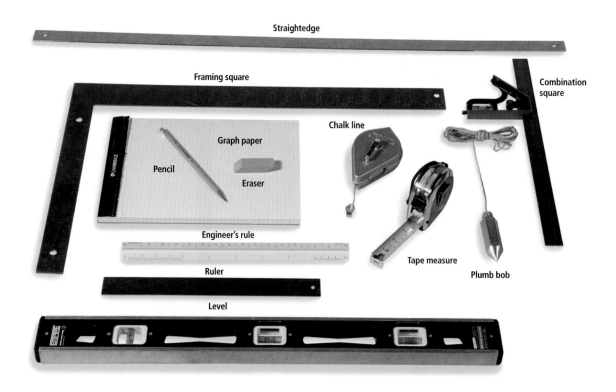

Straightedge
Framing square
Combination square
Graph paper
Pencil
Eraser
Chalk line
Engineer's rule
Ruler
Tape measure
Plumb bob
Level

TILING A FIREPLACE

One of the goals of setting tile is to lay out the job in a way that minimizes the need to cut tile. But at the very least you will need to cut tiles for corners and around fixtures.

Tile-cutting tools range from the slow and tedious to the fast and furious. Deciding which tools you need is largely a matter of the size of your project and the number of cuts required.

A snap cutter is similar to a handheld glass cutter, except it is mounted on a guide bar. Various models operate differently, but all follow a basic two-step approach. First, the tile is set in the cutter and scored along the snap line. Then, the handle is pressed down to snap the tile along the line.

Tile nippers resemble pliers, but they are equipped with carbide-tipped edges. They are indispensable for making small notches and curves in tile. They can also be used for breaking off pieces of tile that have

been scored on a snap cutter. Nippers usually leave a rough edge. Use a rubbing stone to smooth sharp edges. A rod saw is a strip of tungsten carbide that fits into a standard hacksaw body. It's a slow but handy way to cut tight curves. A faster option for making small cuts is a power diamond-tipped cutter.

A wet saw is a power tool that quickly makes smooth, straight cuts in tile and other masonry. Wet saws are equipped with a pump that sprays water to cool the blade and remove chips. They are messy, but not particularly dangerous or difficult to use. In fact you might enjoy watching how easily the blade cuts its way through a piece of tile, marble, or granite.

For drilling holes use a carbide-tipped hole saw mounted on an electric or a cordless power drill.

WHY BUY WHEN YOU CAN RENT?

New home improvement projects offer the perfect excuse to add new tools to your collection. However some tiling tools are so specialized that you won't use them again until your next tiling job. Buying 1 too many tools can quickly destroy your project budget. Tool rental stores offer a variety of tools, many specifically chosen for do-it-yourselfers needing special tools for a short period of time. For tiling projects it's especially smart to rent power tools, such as a wet saw or a diamond-tipped cutter. Also check with your tile supplier. Often the store will lend customers tools at no charge if the tiles were purchased there.

Wet saw

Cordless power drill

Snap cutter

Heavy-duty electric drill

Carbide-tipped hole saw

Hacksaw

Rod saw blade

Nippers

Rubbing stone

Diamond-tipped cutter

SELECTING INSTALLATION TOOLS

For mixing thinset mortar and grout, you need a sturdy bucket. An empty, clean drywall-compound bucket will suffice for relatively small jobs, but a mortar-mixing box is better for larger jobs. A mortar mixer is a great time saver for mixing two or more gallons of thinset mortar or grout. The mixer is mounted on an electric drill chuck like a drill bit.

Notched trowels have two smooth sides for spreading adhesive and two notched sides for combing the adhesive to the right depth. Check the tile and adhesive manufacturer's recommendations for the proper notch size.

You'll need a beater block to press the tiles evenly into the adhesive. Use a piece of 2× lumber covered with terry cloth or buy a rubber-faced model. With saltillo pavers and other irregular tiles, use a rubber mallet instead.

A canvas drop cloth readily absorbs moisture and has enough heft to protect surfaces from dropped tiles. Use masking tape to cover plumbing fixtures.

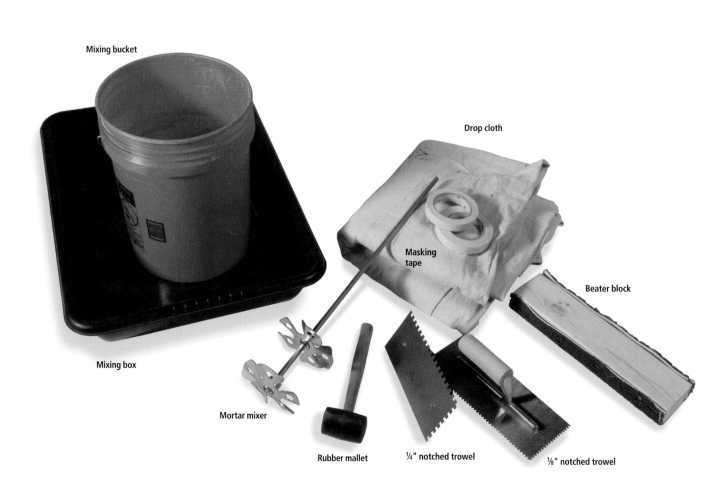

Mixing bucket

Drop cloth

Masking tape

Beater block

Mixing box

Mortar mixer

Rubber mallet

¼" notched trowel

⅛" notched trowel

CHOOSING GROUTING TOOLS

After tiles have been set, the next step is spreading grout. A grouting float is a rubber-backed trowel used for pressing the grout into the joints. It also removes excess grout from the tiling surface, although a squeegee may be more thorough. A mason's trowel is handy for finishing grout joints, although you also can use a putty knife or the handle of an old toothbrush. A margin trowel is used to mix small batches and for scooping adhesive or grout onto the setting surface. A grout bag is useful when you need to force grout into joints that can't be reached easily with a grout float.

Good-quality sponges are best for cleaning grout off the tile surface. Look for sponges made especially for tiling work. Use cheesecloth to remove the haze left on the tile after the grout has set for awhile. For applying caulk and sealant around edges, you will need a caulking gun.

CAUTION

SAFETY EQUIPMENT

Installing tile is not a particularly dangerous occupation, especially if you exercise common sense and follow a few basic safety practices. When using power tools or cutting tile with hand tools, protect your eyes with safety glasses. Plug power tools into an outlet or extension cord equipped with a ground-fault circuit interrupter (GFCI). When mixing and handling adhesive and grout, wear a charcoal-filter mask and rubber gloves.

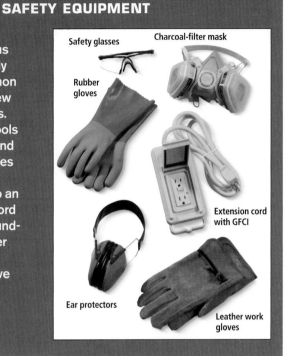

Safety glasses

Charcoal-filter mask

Rubber gloves

Extension cord with GFCI

Ear protectors

Leather work gloves

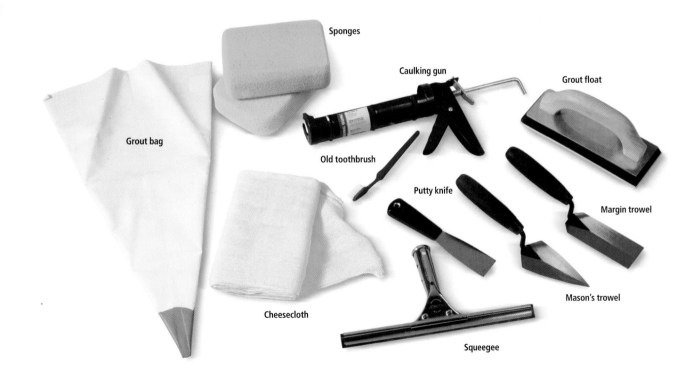

Sponges

Caulking gun

Grout float

Grout bag

Old toothbrush

Putty knife

Margin trowel

Cheesecloth

Mason's trowel

Squeegee

USING TILE SPACERS

The space between tiles serves two important functions: It provides room for the grout essential to any tile job, and it allows for some creativity in your design. You can change the look of a finished tile installation significantly by changing the width of the grout joint or by altering the color of the grout.

Tile spacers are small pieces of plastic used to ensure consistent width of the grout joints. They come in a variety of sizes and shapes to match different types of tile and tile installations. Many types of ceramic tile today are self-spacing, that is, they have small lugs along their sides that ensure proper spacing. If you use self-spacing tiles, you need not use tile spacers unless you prefer a wider grout joint than the lugs allow.

PURCHASE MANUFACTURED SPACERS.

Buy plastic tile spacers from your tile supplier. They are available in sizes from $\frac{1}{16}$ inch to $\frac{1}{2}$ inch. X-shaped spacers are the most common. They are placed at each corner. Though less common, plain spacers often are preferred for spacing and holding wall tiles firmly in place.

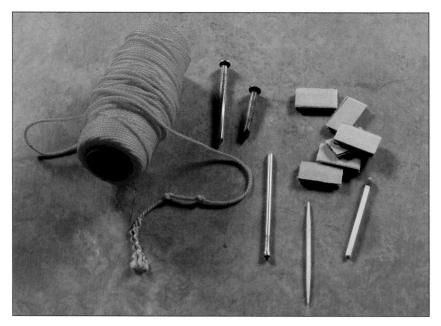

MAKE YOUR OWN SPACERS.

Plastic spacers are one of the least expensive materials used for tile installation. But for a small job or in a pinch, you may need to resort to an alternative. Look for objects that have a consistent size, such as wooden matchsticks, toothpicks, or nails. Nylon cord can be used over a long run. Remember to remove the spacers before grouting.

SELECTING ADHESIVES

The setting adhesive bonds the bottom of the tile with the setting bed. Recent improvements in setting adhesives make it easy for do-it-yourselfers to set tile with professional results. Although adhesives fall into the broad categories of organic mastic and thinset mortar, in reality there are many types of products and manufacturers. The first step in choosing an adhesive is to determine what kind of installation you are doing (wet or dry? indoors or outdoors? floor or wall?) and to what substrate the tile will be applied.

Organic mastics are popular because they require no mixing. However they are not suitable for areas exposed to heat or for exterior installations. Thinset mortars usually are mixed by the installer. A variety of thinset additives are available to create an adhesive best suited to specific installations. The chart below offers general guidelines.

BUY READY-MIXED ORGANIC MASTIC.

Organic mastic is a premixed adhesive that is easy to use. It is especially popular for use on walls because it develops tack more quickly than mortar, so tiles will not slip when set in place.

MIX YOUR OWN THINSET MORTAR.

Thinset mortar requires more work than organic mastic, but offers superior bonding strength and flexibility.

CHOOSING THINSET MORTARS

Type	Description and Uses
Water-mixed mortar	Also referred to as dry-set mortar, this is a blend of portland cement, sand, and additives. Mix with water.
Latex- and acrylic-mixed mortar	Also referred to as latex mortar, this mortar is similar to water-mixed mortar but has latex or acrylic added to it. The additives improve adhesion and reduce water absorption; they may be premixed with the mortar in dry form or added as a liquid by the installer. It's an excellent choice for wet and dry installations.
Epoxy mortar	This is a mixture of sand, cement, and liquid resins and hardeners. It's costly but effective with any setting material and is a good choice when the substrate is incompatible with other adhesives.
Medium-bed mortar	This adhesive remains stronger than regular thinset mortar when applied in layers of more than ¼ inch. It's useful with tiles that do not have uniform backs, such as handmade tiles.

A tile installation is only as good as the surface to which it is applied. Investing in adequate materials for the setting bed is as important as buying the right tile for your project. Tiled floors, in particular, require an extremely stiff setting bed; any imperfection in the subfloor can crack tiles and ruin your project.

You may be able to set the tile over an existing subfloor or wall surface, or you may want to add a layer or two of setting material to ensure a stiff and durable installation. The introduction of cement-based and gypsum-based backerboard has dramatically simplified tile installations without compromising strength and durability. Previously, tile was applied over thick beds of mortar, almost exclusively by trained professionals. The process was time consuming and required skill and experience.

MORTAR-BED INSTALLATIONS

Modern thinset mortars are typically applied in a layer only ⅛ to ¼ inch thick; that's how they get their name. Traditional (mudset) tile installations use thick mortar as the setting bed. Mortar, with wire-mesh reinforcement, is poured over tar paper to a thickness of 1 to 2 inches. Then the tiles are set on the mortar before it cures. Mortar-bed installations are strong and particularly useful on shower floors.

Moisture-resistant wallboard

Cement backerboard

Gypsum-based backerboard

Concrete slab

Gypsum wallboard (drywall)

Plywood

CHOOSE A SETTING BED.

Drywall (regular or moisture-resistant) is a suitable setting bed only in dry areas; for a stronger setting bed, use two layers.

Backerboard often is called cement board, although some products contain no cement. Sold in varying thicknesses and sizes, backerboard is easy to install and provides a ready-made surface for setting tile. Cement-based backerboard has a mesh coat and is cut using a carbide-tipped scoring tool. Gypsum-based backerboard can be cut with a utility knife.

Concrete slabs (old or newly poured) are ideal setting beds for tile floors. With suitable adhesives tile can be installed over plywood.

SELECTING GROUT

Grout is a mortar used to fill the joints between tiles. It stiffens the tile installation and helps prevent moisture from penetrating the joint. Grout usually is sold with all of the dry ingredients mixed together; the installer adds the liquid. It is also available in caulking-gun tubes with all of the wet and dry ingredients already mixed and ready for application.

Grout not only seals joints, it plays an important role in the overall design. The width and color of the grout joint can radically alter the finished look of a tile installation. Choose a grout color to complement, match, or contrast with the tile. Increase or decrease the joint size to provide the most appropriate balance for the size of the room.

CHOOSING GROUT

Type	Description and Uses
Plain grout	Also referred to as unsanded grout, it is a mixture of portland cement and additives chosen to achieve specific characteristics. It is used for grout joints of $\frac{1}{16}$ inch or less. It's also recommended for absorptive tile and marble.
Sanded grout	This is similar to plain grout but has sand added. It is used for grout joints greater than $\frac{1}{16}$ inch. The ratio between sand and cement varies, depending on the size of the joint.
Epoxy grout	This grout contains epoxy resin and hardener. It's used when chemical and stain resistance are required or where high temperatures are likely.
Colored grout	Offered in premixed packages in a wide assortment of colors and formulations, colored grout can usually be found to match any need and fill any typical grout joint. Natural grout can be used if you prefer the look of cement.
Mortar	This is similar to sanded grout but is used for joints between brick pavers, slate, or other masonry materials.
Premixed grout	Some grouts are available premixed and ready to use out of the container. Choices are smaller and the cost is high, but it may be a good choice for small jobs.

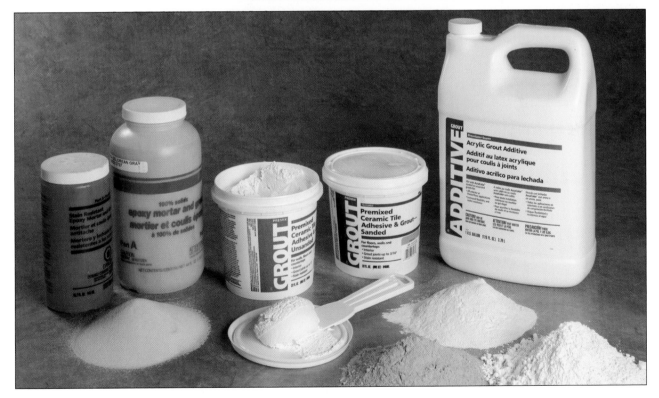

KNOW YOUR GROUT.

Grout and tile are the two visible materials on a tiled surface. A good tile installation requires a good grouting job. Use the best ingredients, mix them right, and apply the grout so it completely fills the joints between tiles. Although tile is completely inflexible, you can achieve some flexibility in the grout joints by adding latex or acrylic additives to the grout. Additives also can increase water and stain resistance. When grout joints begin to fail, they should be repaired immediately or water damage could occur behind the tile.

SELECTING MEMBRANES

In addition to backerboard or other bed materials (see page 116), some installations call for the use of a membrane. The two types are waterproofing membranes and isolation membranes.

Waterproofing membranes are used to prevent moisture from penetrating through the surface, usually from the grout joints. If water will often sit on your floor tiles, or if your wall tiles will be in a room that often becomes very humid, moisture can seep through grout or unglazed tiles and cause serious damage to the substrate and even the structural wood. A sealer (see page 148) may solve the problem for wall tiles, but floor tiles that will get soaked need a membrane.

Tar paper (felt paper saturated with tar) has long been the standard waterproofing membrane. Polyethylene sheeting is another inexpensive option.

The most effective waterproofing membrane is chlorinated polyethylene (CPE), a strong and thick sheet joined to the substrate with adhesive. Liquid membranes are applied with a trowel or brush.

The function of an isolation membrane is to protect the tiled surface from damage due to movement in the underlying surface. Use one when you tile over an existing floor that shows signs of movement from seasonal changes or settling of the house. Chlorinated polyethylene sheets are often used as isolation membranes.

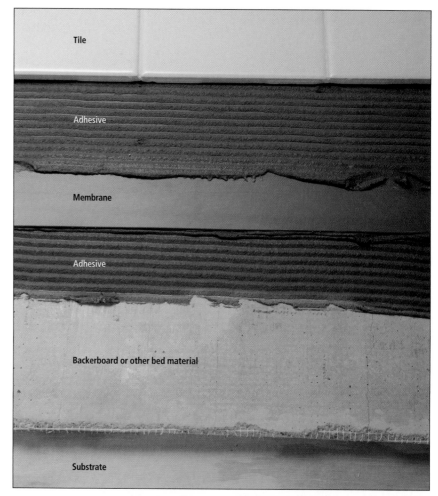

Tile

Adhesive

Membrane

Adhesive

Backerboard or other bed material

Substrate

TAR PAPER WATERPROOFING.

Asphalt-impregnated builder's felt is an inexpensive and easy-to-install membrane. It is sold in rolls of varying widths and lengths and can be stapled or nailed to studs or drywall.

CPE WATERPROOFING.

Chlorinated polyethylene (CPE) is a durable and flexible product that offers the best water resistance of any available membrane. It is particularly effective on floors that will be wet on a regular basis.

CHOOSING CAULK AND SEALERS

Tiles may last centuries, but a tile installation needs regular maintenance to last through the years. Some components of the installation need to be replaced or renewed every few years. Caulk refers to a variety of flexible products used to fill joints that should not be grouted for one reason or another. Sealers are protective coatings applied over the entire tiled surface or all the grout lines; they prevent staining and protect tile and grout from water infiltration.

The best choice for a long-lasting, mildew-free joint in high-moisture installations is silicone caulk. Latex caulk is not suitable for tile jobs. Use siliconized acrylic caulk in areas exposed to only minimal moisture. Tub-and-tile caulk contains a mildewcide, but it does not always work well.

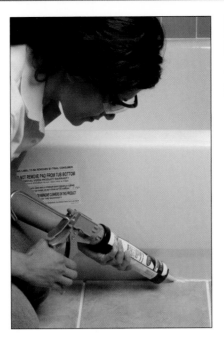

WHERE TO CAULK.

Use caulk instead of grout in expansion joints (see below), between dissimilar materials, and around penetrations in the tiled surface such as between tiles and a sink. Like grout, caulk is available in sanded and plain formulations and in colors that match the grout. Caulk tubes used with a caulk gun are the easiest to use. Buy a squeeze tube for small jobs.

TILE AND GROUT SEALERS

Sealers are used on unglazed tile and stone products.
They are also applied to grout. Penetrating sealers are intended to be absorbed beneath the surface of the tile and grout. They reduce the absorbency of the surface without necessarily adding a sheen. Coating sealers are formulated to remain on the surface, where they generally add a glossy or semiglossy sheen. Use a grout sealer on a wall with glazed tile. It will keep your grout watertight and make it easier to clean. Usually, you must wait two weeks after tile installation before applying grout sealer.

EXPANSION JOINTS

Tile and grout generally don't expand and contract with seasonal and temperature changes, but the materials beneath and around them may. Expansion joints are safety features that anticipate that movement and prevent the tile and grout from being damaged by it. On most installations expansion joints are intended to look like grout joints, but they are filled with a flexible material such as silicone caulk.

Use expansion joints around the perimeters of all tile installations, especially where the tile edges meet a different material. Use them where floors meet walls, countertops meet backsplashes, and where tile meets wood or another material. Any runs of tile on a floor that exceed 24 feet must be interrupted with an expansion joint.

The most typical method of creating an expansion gap is to leave a $\frac{1}{4}$-inch joint between the tile and the adjoining surface, then fill the joint with caulk. The setting bed should also be designed with expansion joints.

ASSESSING SUBSTRATES

The substrate of a floor or wall includes the setting bed (see page 116) and any other layers beneath the tile surface. Even if tile adheres firmly to its setting bed, it won't last long if that setting bed isn't part of a completely sound and sturdy substrate.

The structural needs of your substrate may change when you add a new type of surface. For example if you are planning to install ceramic tile on a floor that currently is covered with resilient sheet flooring, you will be adding a lot of weight to the underlying framing. If you doubt that the joists and subfloor are strong enough, consult a professional.

A quick way to tell if a floor is firm enough to handle ceramic tile: Jump on it. If it feels springy, there's a good chance that your tiles or grout lines will crack in time. Add a layer of plywood or backerboard to strengthen it, or consult a professional to be sure.

Walls should be firm to the touch. New tiles will not add significant strength.

SUBSTRATE RECOMMENDATIONS

Substrate	Preparation
Exposed joists	Verify that the framing will support the new floor. Install ¾-inch CDX plywood. Install backerboard or underlayment-grade plywood.
Concrete slab	Repair cracks or low spots in the concrete. Ensure that the slab is flat, clean, and dry. Roughen the surface to improve adhesion.
Finished floor	Verify that the framing will support the new floor. If necessary remove the finish flooring. Install backerboard or underlayment-grade plywood over a suitable subfloor, or over the old finish flooring.
Wall paneling	Remove thin sheet paneling. Install backerboard, plywood, or drywall.
Drywall	Scrape away any loose paint and roughen the surface with sandpaper. Clean the surface, or apply deglosser. Add a second layer of drywall for added strength.
Masonry or plaster walls	Repair cracks and level indentations. Ensure that the surface is sound, not soft and crumbling or springy when pressed. Clean the surface, or apply deglosser.

WOOD FLOOR SUBSTRATE.

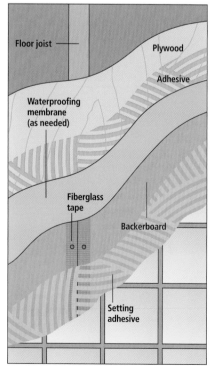

Floor joist — Plywood — Adhesive — Waterproofing membrane (as needed) — Fiberglass tape — Backerboard — Setting adhesive

CONCRETE FLOOR SUBSTRATE.

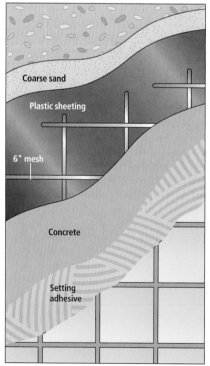

Coarse sand — Plastic sheeting — 6" mesh — Concrete — Setting adhesive

WALL SUBSTRATE.

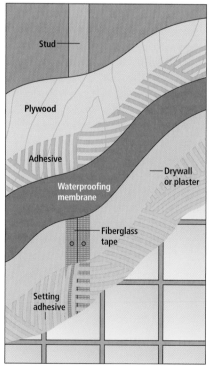

Stud — Plywood — Adhesive — Drywall or plaster — Waterproofing membrane — Fiberglass tape — Setting adhesive

CALCULATING MATERIALS

Before you go shopping for tile and setting materials, determine how much of each material you need. Fortunately that doesn't mean you have to count every tile you intend to install. Tiling materials are usually sold by the square foot, so for most jobs all you have to do is measure the surface to be tiled and take that number to the store.

Buy more tile than you plan to use. Expect to break a few tiles and to need a few more than anticipated. It's handy to have a few extra tiles should you need any replacements someday. Get an extra 10 percent more than your estimate.

Where to buy

Tile and setting materials are widely available. Small lumber yards and hardware stores may carry a limited selection, while home centers and tile outlets offer a much wider choice. It pays to shop around because prices and selection can vary significantly. Of course you should shop for a good price, but also look for a retailer who is knowledgeable and willing to answer questions. A little good advice might save you plenty of time and money. Be sure to ask about the store's policy on returns. In the event that you buy considerably more than you need, you should be able to return unopened boxes and packages for a refund.

Metrics

Tiles are manufactured and sold all over the world. The tiles you choose may have been manufactured to a metric size, which was then rounded off to inches. So, for example, you may have a "13-inch" Italian tile that actually measures 13³⁄16 inches.

DETERMINE SQUARE FOOTAGE.

If you are tiling a single rectangular surface, simply measure the width and the length (in feet) and multiply the two numbers to determine the square footage. For multiple surfaces calculate each one separately, then add the results. When a door or a window interferes, include it in your initial calculation, then find the square footage of the obstruction and subtract it from the overall total.

If you will be installing large, expensive tiles, make a drawing of your space, with exact dimensions, and take it to your dealer, who can help you determine the most economical layout.

ESTIMATING GROUT AND ADHESIVES

The amount of grout you need depends on the size of the tiles and on the width and depth of the grout joint. Packages of grout often include tables for estimating the amount needed. This chart gives you a rough idea of how many square feet can be covered with 1 pound of grout. The figures should be treated only as estimates, but they do show how much the coverage changes depending on tile size.

Substrate	Joint Width	Coverage per Pound of Grout
2×2×¼"	1⁄16"	24 square feet
4¼×4¼×5⁄16"	1⁄16"	16 square feet
4¼×4¼×5⁄16"	⅛"	8 square feet
6×6×¼"	1⁄16"	28 square feet
6×6×¼"	⅛"	14 square feet
12×12×⅜"	1⁄16"	37 square feet

When applied with the trowel-notch size recommended by the manufacturer, one gallon of adhesive will cover 30 to 50 square feet of wall and 20 to 40 square feet of floor.

When tiling floors or installing wall tiles down to the floor line, remove baseboard trim. If the baseboard is trimmed with shoe molding (a thin, rounded strip attached to the floor), you probably need only remove the shoe, leaving the baseboard in place, when tiling the floor. If you plan to reuse the trim, take care not to damage it as you remove it. Insert a thin pry bar or stiff putty knife to lift the shoe or pull the baseboard from the wall. Gradually work your way along the molding until it comes off. Mark the backs of the pieces to help you remember where they go. Remove as many obstacles as possible so you will not have to make many precise tile cuts. When preparing to tile a floor, set a tile on the floor and use it as a guide for cutting the bottoms of door casing molding.

If you are tiling a bathroom, remember that removing and resetting the toilet is easier and will lead to a much cleaner-looking job than if you try to tile around it. (Be sure to stuff a rag in the closet flange

to prevent sewer gas from backing up into the bathroom.) You may want to remove the vanity as well as doors. (You may also need to trim the doors after the tile is installed.)

When preparing to tile walls, remove electrical outlet covers (the outlet box may have to be adjusted before replacing the covers) and

fixtures. Sinks and appliances may have to be removed, depending on your installation. Because the tiles add thickness to the wall, it is usually best to leave window and door casings in place. Keep dust and odors from spreading throughout the house by taping plastic sheeting over doorways. Cover vents with plastic as well.

PREPARING SURFACES TO BE TILED

Floors
- Remove the original flooring, if it is not firmly stuck to the subfloor, if it is uneven, or if the thinset mortar will not adhere to it.

- Make sure that the subfloor is at least 1⅛-inches thick and composed of suitable materials (usually a combination of plywood, backerboard, or concrete).

- If a plywood floor seems loose in spots, drive nails or screws through it into floor joists. Fill low spots in the subfloor, then smooth the surface and clean it thoroughly.

Walls
- Remove wallpaper, thin paneling, or anything that flexes when you press it.

- When tiling over new drywall, you don't need to tape the joints, but, level and seal the surface with a thin coat of compound applied with the flat side of a trowel.

- Scrape away loose paint.

- Lightly sand glossy surfaces to remove the sheen.

- Patch holes and cracks, and sand smooth.

- Thoroughly clean the wall and allow it to dry.

Countertops
- Remove sink or faucets, and other obstacles.

- Remove old tile, if it exists.

- To tile over a square-edged laminated countertop that is sound, give it a thorough sanding and remove the backsplash.

- If you have a post-form countertop with curved edges, remove it and install a new substrate of plywood and backerboard.

- Make sure the substrate is thick enough for trim pieces, and that the trim won't prevent drawers from opening.

SELECTING ADHESIVES

Tile looks best when it is set in a straight line and at least appears to be square and level with adjacent surfaces. Laying out the installation is the most important step for ensuring such an outcome. Tile is an unforgiving material, and floors and walls are rarely as square and level as you might think—or hope. One of the secrets to a successful layout, therefore, is learning how to make minor, unnoticeable adjustments to the installation. The other secret is to plan for as few cut tiles as possible. Adjust the layout to minimize cuts and hide those cut tiles along less conspicuous walls and under baseboard trim. Don't be surprised if your house exceeds some of the tolerances recommended here. Carefully planning, preparation, and handling of materials can overcome almost any irregularity.

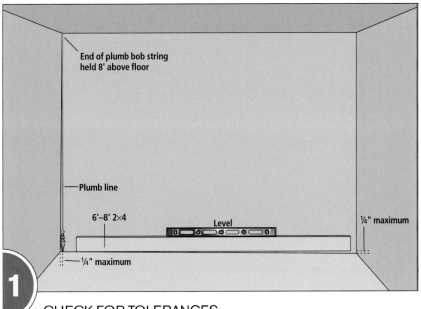

End of plumb bob string held 8' above floor

Plumb line

6'–8' 2×4

Level

¼" maximum

¼" maximum

1 CHECK FOR TOLERANCES.

Check tiling surfaces for square, level, and plumb using the techniques shown below. If a surface is out of alignment in excess of the amounts shown above, the best solution is to change the surfaces—for instance, fur out a wall or shim up a subfloor. If this is not feasible, make the unevenness less visible by avoiding narrow tile pieces at the corner. You might be able to split the difference, making two edges slightly out of line instead of having one edge that is way off.

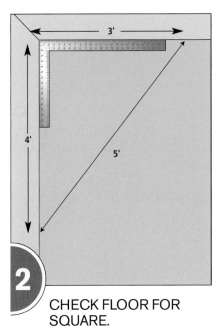

3'

4'

5'

2 CHECK FLOOR FOR SQUARE.

For small areas, check the squareness of the floor by setting a framing square at inside and outside corners. For larger areas, use the 3-4-5 method: Measure along one wall exactly 3 feet from the corner, and along the other wall 4 feet. If the distance between those spots is exactly 5 feet, the floor is square.

3 CHECK FLOOR FOR LEVEL.

Use a 2- or 4-foot level to check along each wall. To check for level over a longer span, place the level on the edge of a straight 6- or 8-foot board. If the floor is only slightly out of level, and you are not planning to run tile up the wall, this should not affect your installation.

4 CHECK WALLS FOR PLUMB.

Place a level vertically on the wall at various spots, or use a plumb bob. Set the level horizontally on the wall to see how flat it is (you can also stretch a string tightly along the wall). A wavy wall, even if it is plumb, should be corrected before tiling.

Laying out the job *(continued)*

PLANNING FOR FOCAL POINTS

When you walk into a room for the first time, chances are there is something there that catches your eye immediately. As you stand in the room, other areas may become more noticeable. It might be another doorway, a fireplace, a window, counters, or appliance groupings. Plan your layout so the installation looks best in these focal areas. Cut tiles placed around a sink should all be of equal size, for example. If your floor is out of square so you must have a line of cut tiles that grows progressively smaller, plan ahead so it will be in an area that is not a focal point. Use perpendicular lines and full tiles at focal points.

5 ESTABLISH REFERENCE LINES.

Accurate reference lines are critical to the success of a tile installation. Trace around a piece of plywood with two factory edges, or chalk two lines that are perfectly perpendicular. You will place the first tile at the intersection; this tile establishes the alignment and position of the rest of the tiles. (For more information on how to plot reference lines, refer to specific projects in the "Tile Projects" chapter.)

LAYING OUT AN L-SHAPED ROOM.

Often, the outside corner of an L-shaped room will be a focal point, so start there. Here's the simplest way to lay it out: From the corner extend two straight lines along the floor to the opposing wall. Plan to set three full tiles at the corner, then extend the layout. However this will not work if the outside corner is seriously out of square. Also if this method results in very small pieces along a wall, it may be best to modify it.

USING TILE SCRAPS

By making adjustments in your layout, you can save some money. That's because you can plan ahead to use as many of your tile cutoffs as possible. As explained below, avoid using tiles that are less than half size. There are times when you won't have a choice, however, especially if you are tiling an oddly shaped room or an irregular surface. In those cases try to use tiles that have already been cut rather than wasting full ones. Tile scraps can also be used for mosaic installations.

6 DRY-SET THE TILES.

With reference lines drawn, you can measure from the lines to the walls and calculate how the tiles will be arranged. However, the safest method is to set tiles in place along the reference lines or use a layout stick (see page 110).

For this dry run, don't use any adhesive, but be sure to space the tiles properly. Take your time, and find out how each edge will look. Don't hesitate to change the entire layout if it will make for a more attractive appearance.

HIDING CUT TILES.

One big advantage of a careful and thorough layout is that you can plan where cut tiles will go. A simple rule of thumb is to place cut tiles in the least visible areas. On a floor installation, for example, one wall may be largely covered with furniture. If you place cut tiles under the furniture, they are not likely to be seen. On other installations, you may prefer to adjust the layout so it has evenly sized cut tiles along the opposing surfaces.

▼ CAUTION

AVOID NARROW TILES

One of the golden rules of tile setting is to use as many full tiles as possible. Another rule is to avoid using tiles that have been cut in size by more than half. Sometimes those rules are easier to remember than to follow. Then, follow the most important rule: avoid using very narrow tiles. Not only are they unattractive, but they also may not adhere properly. When your layout reveals the need for one row of very thin tiles, make an adjustment. Plan to cut tiles along two rows rather than one; that way they won't be so narrow.

CUTTING WITH A CIRCULAR SAW

Whether crosscutting 2×4s, ripping plywood, or cutting tiles or bricks with a masonry blade, you'll do the job better if you follow a few basic rules for using a circular saw.

Whenever you cut allow the saw to reach full operating speed, then slowly push the blade into the wood. Some carpenters look at the blade as they cut; others rely on the gunsight notch. Choose the method that suits you best. Avoid making slight turns as you cut. Instead find the right path, and push the saw through the material smoothly. It will take some practice before you can do this consistently. This is a powerful tool with sharp teeth, so take care. It demands your respect. Support the material to avoid having the saw bind and possibly kick back at you. Don't wear long sleeves or position your face near the blade.

SUPPORT THE MATERIAL PROPERLY.

A well-supported board results in clean, safe cuts. If the scrap piece is short, support the board on the nonscrap side. If the scrap is long, it could bind the blade or splinter as it falls away at the end of the cut, so support it in four places.

SQUARE THE BLADE.

Make certain the saw is unplugged. Turn the saw upside down, hold a square against the blade, and adjust it. (Be sure to position the square between the teeth.) Cut some scrap pieces and check to make sure the saw cuts squarely through the thickness of the board.

ALIGN THE BLADE WITH THE CUT LINE.

Once you have drawn an accurate cutoff line and have properly supported the board, position the saw blade on the scrap side of the line. The teeth on most all-purpose blades (not carbide-tipped) are offset in an alternating pattern. When preparing to cut, look at a tooth that points toward the cutoff line.

MAKE A PLUNGE CUT.

Use a plunge cut, also called a pocket cut, to make a hole or slit in the middle of a board or sheet. Set the blade to the correct depth. Retract the safety guard and tilt the saw forward, setting the front of the baseplate on the stock. Start the saw and lower it slowly into the cut line until the base rests on the stock. Complete the cut.

An electric drill enables you not only to drill a hole of about any size with ease but also to drive screws into wood or metal, buff and grind, and even mix mortar or paint.

Many craftsmen keep two drills on hand—one for drilling pilot holes and the other for driving screws. That way they don't waste time changing bits. A drill with a keyless chuck speeds up a bit change, although you may find bits slip during heavy-duty tasks.

In addition to the bits shown at right, purchase a magnetic sleeve that holds inexpensive screwdriver bits. This simple tool will make driving screws nearly as easy as pounding nails.

CHOOSING A DRILL

Avoid buying a cheap drill with a ¼-inch chuck. It will not have the power you need and may soon burn out. A good drill will be variable-speed and reversing (VSR), will have a ⅜-inch chuck, and will pull at least 3 amps. Look for a long cord that flexes more like rubber than plastic.

Choose a heavy-duty, ½-inch drill if you will be using it to mix mortar. A smaller drill can burn out quickly while churning this thick substance.

A cordless drill can make your work go more easily, but only if it is powerful enough to do most things that a corded drill can do. A 12-volt model handles general purpose chores; an 18-volt drill can handle heavy duties.

A hammer drill is useful if you need to drill a number of holes in concrete.

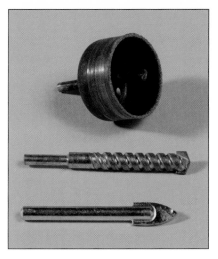

CHOOSE THE RIGHT BIT.

Use standard twist or spade bits for boring through wood. A carbide-tipped masonry bit drills through concrete or brick. Use a carbide-tipped hole saw for larger holes. A spear-point ceramic tile bit will make a hole in tile or glass with less risk of cracking it.

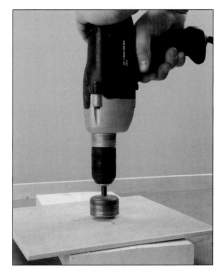

USE A HOLE SAW.

Cutting a hole in the middle of a tile is easy to do with a carbide-tipped hole saw. Measure to the center of the hole (you will need to make two measurements), and place the tile on a flat surface that you don't mind damaging. Nick the center point to keep the starter bit from wandering. Keep the drill perpendicular as you drill and don't press too hard.

DRILL THROUGH CERAMIC TILE.

Nick the surface of the tile just enough so the bit will not wander as you drill. Keep the bit and the hole lubricated with a few drops of oil. Use a masonry bit or ceramic tile bit, such as the one shown above.

DRILL INTO MASONRY AND CONCRETE.

Use a masonry bit when drilling masonry surfaces. Usually brick is easy to drill into and concrete is more difficult. Check the bit often to make sure it's not overheating. Stop if you see smoke. Spraying the bit with window cleaner as you work keeps the bit cool, and the foaming action brings debris up and out of the hole.

Tiling
TECHNIQUES

Several tiling techniques are common to all tiling projects, whether it be a floor, wall, or countertop installation. Familiarizing yourself with these techniques before you delve into your project will save you time during installation. Consider making a few notes to refer to while you work.

Most tiling projects require a backerboard, a ready-made surface for setting tile. On pages 130 and 131 you will find instructions for cutting and installing this substrate. All tiling projects require an adhesive—using the right adhesive for the job, mixing it to the proper consistency, and spreading it for good coverage are important techniques discussed on pages 132 and 133.

Depending on the type of tile and the project, you will inevitably need to cut tile. There are several different tools for cutting and trimming tile, including a wet saw, tile nippers, and a snap cutter (see pages 134 and 135). Once the tile is cut, it must be set. Pages 136 and 137 will show you how to properly set tile. In addition mosaic tiles, handmade pavers, and stone tiles all require special attention and instructions (see pages 138–141).

Finally, there are tips on completing the finishing touches: grouting, caulking, and sealing. Premature breakdown in the performance of tile is often due to a poor grouting job. Follow the instructions on pages 142–144 for a flawless grouting job. It is equally important to seal grout and tile, and caulk should be used when tile butts up against another surface (see page 145).

MOSAIC SYMMETRY

Today, mosaic tiles are typically sold in sheets, making them far more user-friendly for installation. This ornate countertop is composed of colorful patterns. If your mosaic sheets come with random colors, play around with the layout before setting in adhesive to create an attractive pattern. See page 138 for more about setting mosaic tile.

FOCAL POINT

Adding a mural to a kitchen backsplash can change or enhance the theme of the entire room. This backsplash incorporates mural tiles and sets the color scheme for kitchen accessories. You should be comfortable with the techniques of trimming and setting tiles prior to starting a project like this. See pages 136–137 for the basics of setting tile.

SMOOTH TRANSITIONS

This is a beautiful example of making a smooth transition from one room to the next. The gray stone tile used in the kitchen is carefully integrated into the design of the dining room. Stone tile will require the use of a wet saw, and a latex-modified thinset mortar will work best for installation. See pages 140–141 for more on working with stone tile.

CUTTING BACKERBOARD

Backerboard usually has to be cut to size before it can be installed. You may also have to drill holes in the board (for pipes or fixtures). If you have ever installed drywall, you will find the score-and-snap method to be very familiar. There are several types of backerboard on the market, and new materials are introduced from time to time. Be sure to follow the manufacturer's instructions if they vary from the process described here. You can cut backerboard with power tools, but it will be messier, not any faster, and may damage your blade or motor.

YOU'LL NEED

TIME: Each cut requires no more than 5–10 minutes.

SKILLS: Measuring, cutting.

TOOLS: Drywall square or straightedge, utility knife or scoring tool, rubbing stone.

1 SCORE THE BOARD.

For cement-based board, measure carefully and mark cutoff lines on both sides of the backerboard. Align a straightedge with the line on one side. Pull the scoring tool along the straightedge; make as many passes as necessary to break through the mesh on the surface. Place the straightedge on the other side and repeat the process. The mesh must be completely severed on each side. (A faster but somewhat riskier method: Proceed as you would for drywall, cutting one side, snapping the cut edge over, then cutting the other side.)

2 SNAP.

Place the backerboard on a flat surface. Press down with your hand on one side of the cut line. With the other hand, lift up just enough to snap the board along the scored edges. Some types of backerboard may break more easily if you elevate the board on one side of the scoring line, then press down.

3 SMOOTH EDGES.

Be careful when handling the cut board. Some types of backerboard may leave a rough edge along the cut line. The best way to smooth the edge is to use a rubbing stone.

USING A HOLE SAW

Cement-based backerboard is often used under tiled surfaces in wet areas. That means you may have to fit it over plumbing protrusions in the wall, countertop, or floor. Most holes can be drilled quickly and effectively using a power drill equipped with a carbide-tipped hole saw. The hole saw should be available where you buy your tile or at any large home center. Another method is to mark and score a circle on both sides of the board, then tap through with a hammer.

INSTALLING BACKERBOARD

If cut correctly, backerboard is fairly easy to install. Each type is installed with screws or nails, then the seams are joined with fiberglass tape and mortar. If you are planning to tile in a wet area, remember to take the proper waterproofing steps. Cement-based backerboard itself is not damaged by moisture, but it is not waterproof. Water can permeate the board and the underlying framing, causing serious damage. For best results install a waterproofing membrane behind the backerboard (see page 118). Use the type of fasteners recommended by the manufacturer. Roofing nails work, but corrosion-resistant screws offer superior holding power. Edges of backerboard must be supported by studs or joists, or glued with construction adhesive to a sound wall surface.

ATTACH TO WALLS.

Attach backerboard directly to bare studs or over an existing layer of drywall. In either case make sure the drywall screws or nails are long enough to penetrate the framing at least ¾ inch.

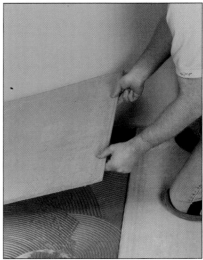

ATTACH TO FLOORS.

Coat the clean subfloor with adhesive applied with a notched trowel. Set the boards so all the joints fall over floor joists. Press the board into the adhesive before fastening with screws.

EXPANSION GAPS BETWEEN BOARDS

One of the most important steps you can take to ensure a long-lasting tile installation is to plan for some movement on and below the finished surface. Expansion gaps, filled with a flexible material, allow for normal movement without jeopardizing the integrity of the tile and grout. Each manufacturer has specific recommendations for expansion gaps around board edges. As a general rule, you should leave a ⅛-inch gap between boards and a ¼-inch gap around bathtubs and shower pans.

FINISH THE JOINTS.

With all boards fastened, apply adhesive-backed fiberglass mesh tape to the joints. Holding a trowel nearly flat, spread adhesive over the tape, pressing it into the mesh. Feather the

edges of the adhesive for a smooth finish. Make sure there are no high spots; shallow low spots are not a problem.

MIXING THINSET MORTAR

With the setting bed placed, cleaned, and marked for the layout, it is time to prepare the adhesive. For tiling walls you will probably use an adhesive that does not have to be mixed. For tiling floors you can use premixed thinset mortar or floor tile adhesive. The thinset mortar you mix yourself will be the strongest (see page 115).

Mixing will be easier if all the ingredients are at room temperature; buy the powder and any additives in advance and store them overnight in a heated part of the house. Mixing can get sloppy, especially if you use a power mixer. Place the bucket in the middle of the area to be tiled, or on top of a drop cloth.

Use a heavy-duty, ½-inch drill for power mixing, because a smaller drill may burn out. Keep a second bucket on hand, about half full of water, for cleaning your mixer.

MIXING BY HAND.

Mix small batches of thinset mortar (less than two gallons) by hand. Use a trowel or a stiff piece of wood, and make sure you scrape the bottom of the bucket as you stir.

USING A MORTAR MIXER.

Mix larger batches with a mortar mixer mounted on a powerful drill. Clamp the bucket with your feet to keep it from spinning. Set the mixer in, and start mixing with short bursts of power, to keep the mixture from spilling over.

HOW MUCH TO MIX?

Like other cement-based adhesives, thinset mortar begins to cure almost as quickly as it is mixed. If you mix too much at once, it may be unusable when you reach the bottom of the bucket. On the other hand, it is a waste of time to mix batches that are too small. Professional tile setters mix enough adhesive to last them somewhere between 30 and 60 minutes. However if you are working in a room with dry air, you may need to mix less. Experiment with progressively larger batches.

ACHIEVING PROPER CONSISTENCY.

It takes some practice and experience to know when the mortar has just the right amount of ingredients. The mix is too loose if it runs off the mixing tool. Add more dry ingredients and mix some more. Lift the mixer again. The mortar is ready when it falls off, but no longer runs off, the mixing tool. If the mortar starts drying out before you've used it up, discard the batch and mix a new one. Adding more liquid at that point will keep the mortar from adhering well.

SPREADING THINSET MORTAR

After mixing the mortar, let it rest for 10 minutes before applying. Scoop a small amount onto the setting surface and comb it with a notched trowel. If the ridges hold their shape and do not flatten out, the batch is ready to spread. Begin spreading mortar at the intersection of your reference lines. Take care not to cover up the lines. Work in small areas. If you've never tiled before, spread only enough to cover 2 or 3 square feet. As you gain experience, you can expand the size of the working area. Packages of thinset mortar refer to the open time—the amount of time you have to set tiles on combed adhesive. Use a margin trowel (see page 113) to scoop adhesive onto the bottom of your notched trowel, or drop dollops of mortar onto the floor and then spread them out. Give the thinset mortar a quick stir from time to time.

1 APPLY THE THINSET MORTAR.

Hold the smooth edge of the trowel at a 30-degree angle to the surface. Press adhesive firmly onto the surface. Use sweeping strokes to spread to a consistent depth. Don't cover reference lines.

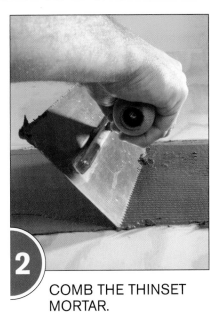

2 COMB THE THINSET MORTAR.

Turn the trowel to the notched edge. Hold the trowel at a 45- to 75-degree angle to form the proper depth of ridge. Comb over the entire surface to produce equally sized ridges.

CAUTION

WORKING WITH EPOXY ADHESIVE

Epoxy-based adhesives are expensive and tricky to use. Fortunately they are usually not needed for residential tile jobs. But if you have a setting bed that is incompatible with other adhesives, or are installing tile in an area likely to receive extreme heat, epoxies may be necessary. Read all instructions carefully. Wear a charcoal-filter mask, work in a well-ventilated area, and avoid skin contact with the mixed solution. Mix epoxy adhesive by hand and carefully follow the manufacturer's instructions about the proportion of wet and dry ingredients.

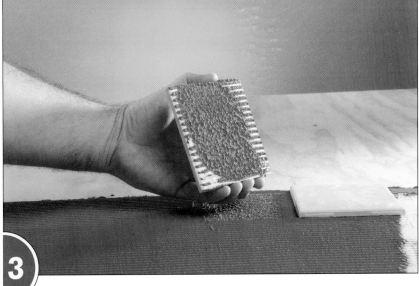

3 CHECK THE COVERAGE.

After spreading and combing a small amount of the mortar, press a tile in place. Twist it a bit so it is set in the adhesive, then pry it up and look at the bottom. About 75 percent of the surface should be covered. If too little adhesive has stuck to the tile bottom, the mixture is probably too dry.

CUTTING TILE

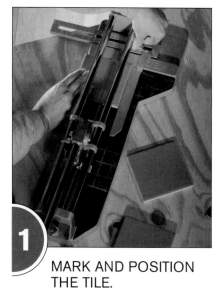

1 MARK AND POSITION THE TILE.

Mark a cut line on the tile with a pencil or felt-tipped pen. Place a tile in the cutter, glazed side up, aligning the cut line with the cutting wheel. Set and lock the fence on the cutter to hold the tile in place.

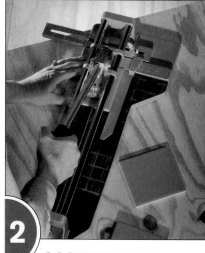

2 SCORE THE TILE.

Hold the tile in place with one hand and the handle with the other. Set the cutting wheel on the top of the tile. Pull or push (depending on your model) the handle while maintaining steady pressure on the tile. Try to score the tile evenly on the first pass.

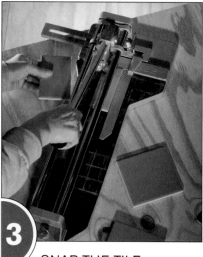

3 SNAP THE TILE.

When the tile has been scored, press back on the handle just enough to snap the tile along the score line. If the tile will not break, the score line was probably incomplete or not deep enough.

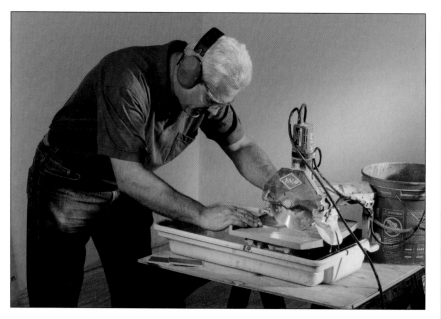

USE A WET SAW.

Wear safety glasses and hearing protection. Make sure the blade is in good condition and that the water bucket is full. Place the tile on the sliding table, and lock the fence to hold the tile in place. Turn the saw on, and make sure water is running onto the blade. Press down on the tile as you slide it through, taking care to keep your fingers out of the way. When the water runs out, refill the bucket; do not cut with the saw for even a few seconds unless water is running onto the blade.

CAUTION

BEWARE OF EDGES

One of the advantages of a wet saw is that it makes very smooth cuts. When using a snap cutter or tile nippers, however, the resulting edges can be razor sharp. After cutting the tile, immediately smooth those edges. Grasp the tile on an uncut edge. Move a rubbing stone back and forth over the cut side, smoothing and rounding over the edge as you go. If you do not have a rubbing stone, you can achieve the same result with carbide-grit sandpaper. Use a sanding block, or wrap the sandpaper around a block of wood.

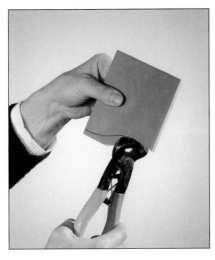

USE TILE NIPPERS FOR A CURVED CUT…

For cuts that are not straight, use a rod saw (see below right), or tile nippers. (Most floor tiles cannot be cut with a rod saw, so you will need to use nippers.) Practice on scrap pieces of tile to get the hang of it. Hold the nippers roughly parallel to the cut line, and bite away small chunks.

FOR A NOTCH…

If the notch will have square corners, use a snap cutter to score at least some of the lines; this will make it a bit easier to nibble precisely up to the lines. Nibbling a notch requires patience. Bite away only a little at a time, or you may break the whole piece.

OR FOR A SLIVER.

Nippers are also useful for very narrow straight cuts when you do not have a wet saw. Use the snap cutter or a glass cutter to score the glaze on the tile. Place the jaws close to, and parallel with, the score line. Take a series of bites along the cut line.

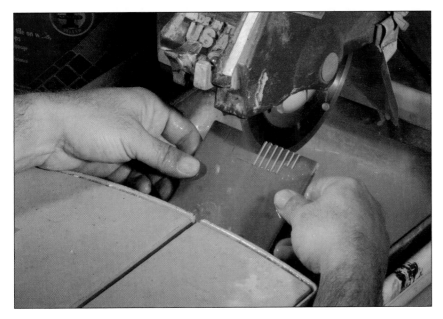

MAKE IRREGULAR CUTS.

Use a wet saw to make irregular cuts that would take a long time to accomplish with nippers. To make a series of closely spaced, parallel cuts with the wet saw, hold the tile in your hands. Rest your hands on the sliding table as you move the tile into the blade. By holding the tile at the correct angle, you can produce a series of cuts that all end at the cut line. Break off the tile pieces with your fingers or nippers, then clean up the cut edge with a rubbing stone.

THE ROD SAW

A rod saw is a cylindrical hacksaw blade made of tungsten carbide. If you are on a tight budget or do not have very many odd-shaped cuts to make, this tool can be a handy accessory. Set the rod saw snugly in the hacksaw body, firmly support the tile, and cut using a sawing motion. With a rod saw you can cut fairly quickly through wall tiles, but it will be rough going—and perhaps impossible—with floor tiles. A rod saw is useful for cutting tight curves.

SETTING TILE

When the adhesive has been combed to the right thickness, immediately begin setting tiles. The most important tile is the first one you set; make sure it aligns perfectly with your layout so the rest of the tiles will fall into place nicely. You will be rewarded at this stage for having spent all that time on the layout. Your reference lines will help guide you through the entire process; take care not to cover them over with adhesive.

Work in sections small enough to set the tiles before the adhesive begins to dry out. Start by spreading adhesive in a 2- to 3-square-foot area; set the tiles and remove excess adhesive before moving on to the next section. With practice you can work in larger sections. If the adhesive begins to skin over, do not set tiles in it. Rather scoop up and discard the adhesive and apply a fresh layer.

Whenever possible set all full tiles first, then set the cut tiles. But also avoid kneeling on top of just-set tiles when laying the cut ones. On a large job, you might want to set all of the full tiles one day, then handle the cut tiles the next day.

Take care not to tile yourself into a corner. Set tiles so you can leave the room without walking on them. Don't disturb floor tiles until the adhesive has cured—preferably overnight.

YOU'LL NEED

TIME: About 1 hour for every 3 to 5 square feet of field tiles; small, complex installations take two to three times as long.

SKILLS: Setting tiles into the adhesive, cutting tiles to fit.

TOOLS: Beater block and hammer, putty knife or trowel, sponge, tile cutter.

1 BEGIN AT THE CORNER.

With the adhesive spread, place the first tile at the intersection of the reference lines. Press and twist it slightly into place, aligning the tile with both lines. Do not slide the tile through the adhesive.

2 FOLLOW THE LAYOUT.

Place another tile next to the first. Use spacers unless the tiles are self-spacing. Press and twist the tile to ensure that it is fully embedded in the adhesive. Accurate placement of the first few tiles is critical.

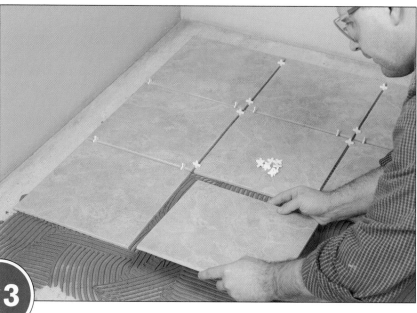

3 FILL IN THE FIELD.

Continue setting tiles along the layout lines in the section. Then set the tiles in the field, working out from the corner. Insert spacers as shown. (Spacers can also be laid flat at the intersection of the grout lines, but must be removed before grouting.)

If the tiles are self-spacing, keep an eye on the gaps between tiles to make sure they remain uniform. Avoid sliding the tiles once they have been set in the adhesive. Check the backs of the tiles from time to time to see that they are adhering properly.

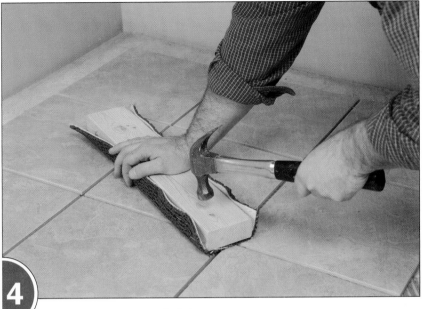

4 USE A BEATER BLOCK.

After setting tiles in one section, use a beater block (see page 112 for tips on making a beater block) to ensure a level surface and full adhesion. Place the beater block so it spans several tiles, and give it a few light taps with a hammer. Make sure each tile gets tapped this way.

5 CLEAN THE JOINTS.

Immediately after setting tiles in each section, go back and remove excess adhesive before it starts to dry. Clean the tile surfaces with a damp sponge, and use a putty knife or margin trowel to remove excess from between tiles.

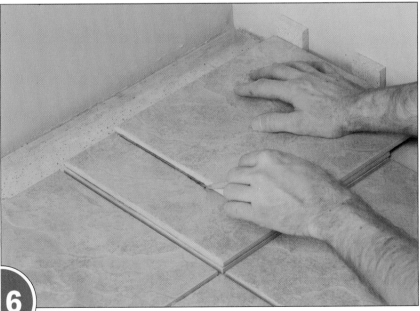

6 CUT TILES LAST.

When all of the full tiles have been set in the field, begin setting cut tiles around the perimeter. Because walls are rarely square, it is usually best to cut one tile at a time. The safest method is to measure each tile "in place." Set the tile to be cut directly on top of the adjacent tile. Then set another full tile on top, two grout joints away from the wall. Use the top tile to mark the cut line.

7 BACK-BUTTERING TILES.

When you are unable to use a trowel to apply the adhesive on the setting surface, back-butter individual tiles: Use a notched trowel or a putty knife, depending on the size of the tile, and spread adhesive on the back. Use enough adhesive so the tile will be level with other tiles.

Historically tile mosaic has been an elaborate decorative technique using small pieces of tile, stone, and shells set one by one to produce unique patterns. Today mosaic tiles are almost always sold in sheets, with small tiles held together by a mesh or paper backing, or with small adhesive dots. These sheets make installation much quicker than setting tiles individually. You can find mosaic tiles in a variety of patterns, glazed and unglazed. Glass mosaic tiles are available in 1-inch squares. Mosaic tiles are particularly suitable for use on floors but are also popular for walls and countertops.

ARRANGING PATTERNS

Sheets of mosaic tiles are sometimes composed of randomly arranged tiles in a variety of colors. This randomness looks best when it has a balance to it; colors should be scattered around the surface, not clumped together. You can control the balance somewhat by planning the arrangement of the tile sheets. Before you start spreading adhesive and setting the tiles, take time to study the patterns on individual sheets. You may find that some sheets look better than others when placed next to each other. Some mosaic sheets are set according to a pattern. In that case install the tiles so you continue, rather than disrupt, the pattern.

SET MOSAIC TILES.

Back-mounted mosaic tiles should be set in thinset adhesive. Because various backing materials perform differently, check with the supplier for any special instructions. Take care to ensure that each individual tile on a sheet is fully embedded in the adhesive. Move a beater block slowly across the whole sheet, lightly tapping it as you go.

CUT MOSAICS.

One advantage of small mosaic tiles is you can often manage an installation without having to cut individual tiles. Use a utility knife to cut strips of tiles away from the sheet. If you do need to fill in spaces with small, cut tiles, remove the tiles from the backing and cut them with a snap cutter or nippers. Back-butter the tiles with adhesive before setting.

WORKING WITH IRREGULARLY SHAPED TILE

Handmade paver tiles lend a pleasing informality to a room. Mexican tiles, called saltillos, are one common choice; they have the added benefit of being very inexpensive. Handmade tiles will not be uniformly shaped; they can vary widely in shape, thickness, size, and color from tile to tile. Choose the tiles by inspecting each one and discarding those with severe blemishes.

Irregularly shaped tiles present several installation challenges. Not only are sizes unpredictable, but some of them may be significantly warped. Tiles of different thicknesses can create a tripping hazard if not installed with care. Since the backs are often not flat, back-butter each tile with adhesive. Handmade tiles cannot be cut easily with a snap cutter; a wet saw is much more effective. Some types require application of a sealer before grouting.

FLOOR LAYOUT FOR IRREGULAR PAVERS.

When the tiles are not of predictably uniform size, the layout becomes less precise. Rather than using plastic spacers, break the layout into a grid. For tiles that are approximately 12 inches square, use chalk lines to make 3-foot squares; each square will hold nine tiles. Dry-fit the tiles first, adjusting the spaces between them by sight. Then set the tiles one square at a time.

1 SET THE TILES.

Comb on thinset mortar (see page 133). For tiles with irregular backs, apply adhesive on the backs as well to ensure an adequate bond. To make sure you can compensate for warped tiles and varying thicknesses, use a trowel with ½-inch notches to spread the adhesive.

2 TAP WITH A MALLET.

With uniform, machine-made pavers, you can use a beater block as described on page 137. With handmade pavers, however, tap on each tile individually. Use a soft mallet, not a hammer. Set a rag on the paver to prevent the mallet from marring the surface.

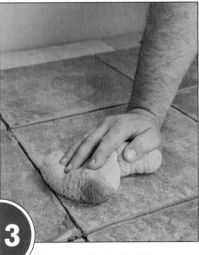

3 CLEAN THE TILES.

Remove mortar that oozes up between the tiles. Take care to keep mortar off the surface of the tiles. Before grouting, clean the tiles with a sponge and water. Apply sealer to unsealed tiles before grouting.

WORKING WITH STONE TILE

Stone tiles are made from stone quarried all over the world. Many types are available, and they vary widely in color and price. Polished stone has a shiny, almost glazelike finish that looks best on walls and interior floors. Honed stone has a smooth, matte finish that does not show wear as much as polished stone. If properly sealed honed tiles can be used in wet areas where polished stone would be too slippery. Flamed stone has a rough finish that is most useful on heavily traveled floors. Most stone is brittle, so the substrate must be strong—at a minimum, backerboard over ¾-inch plywood or a thick mortar bed. Because stone is heavy, be sure your floor joists are strong enough to hold it. Check with an engineer or architect if you are not sure. Cut stone tile with a wet saw, and use a blade suitable for the type of stone you are cutting.

TYPES OF STONE

Type	Description	Pros	Cons
Marble	A limestone that has been changed deep beneath the earth's surface into a hard composition of crystals. Characterized by varied patterns and colors of veins.	Elegant appearance, used in many of the world's most famous buildings; beautiful and long lasting.	Veins add to appeal but weaken the marble. Dark-colored marble can fade in sunlight. Easily scratched and stained.
Granite	Quartz-based stone with a tough, glossy appearance. Colors range from light to dark, with varying patterns and grains.	Harder than marble; resists scratching. Easy to care for; resists acids. Excellent choice for kitchen countertops. Generally very dense and capable of withstanding freeze/thaw cycles.	Quarried all over the world, with varying characteristics from each region. Softer granites can sometimes show wear.
Slate	A rough-surfaced tile that is split, rather than sliced, from quarried stone. Available in slabs or as cut tiles, usually 12 inches square. Gauged slate is ground smooth on the bottom, while ungauged (or cleft) slate is rough on both sides.	Widely available and reasonably priced.	Somewhat brittle, with less range of colors than other stones. Dark slate may fade in sunlight. Irregular surface can produce undesirable flooring. Ungauged slate needs to be set in a thick mortar bed.

MATERIALS TO USE WITH STONE TILE.

Be sure to get the right materials for setting, grouting, and sealing your stone tiles.

Latex-modified thinset mortar works for most installations, but epoxy thinset may be needed. Do not use organic mastics. Marble is somewhat transparent, so use white thinset rather than gray.

With ceramic tile a contrasting grout color is often used as part of the design. With stone tile, especially marble and granite, the objective is usually to minimize or eliminate the visual impact of the grout joints, so the surface resembles a solid whole.

Choose a grout color that closely matches the stone. Use unsanded grout with marble and slate tiles, and epoxy adhesive as grout with closely spaced granite tiles.

Clear sealers can improve the appearance of stone tile and protect it from dirt, water, and stains. Use a low-sheen penetrating sealer on a floor; glossy sealers work well with other surfaces. Choose a sealer recommended for your type of stone. Test it on a scrap tile to make sure it won't discolor your tiles. Granite usually needs no sealer.

SHOPPING FOR STONE

Often the most attractive stones are the weakest because of their deep veins. Stone tiles are often sorted according to their background color, but variations within the sorted colors can be substantial. Look through each box of tiles before you buy. Get extras so you can return tiles that are unsatisfactory. Buy only from a knowledgeable and reputable dealer.

Granite and marble are usually quarried and then manufactured to uniform sizes and thicknesses. Standard tiles are 12 inches square and ⅜ inch thick, with one side polished smooth. To minimize chipping the exposed edges of granite and marble tiles are slightly beveled. The edges are usually so smooth and straight that the grout joint between tiles can be very thin; sometimes the tiles are installed without any grout joints at all. Dry-set before applying adhesive and laying tiles.

YOU'LL NEED

TIME: About 1 day for a 12-foot-long countertop.

SKILLS: Cutting and setting tiles, aligning tiles carefully.

TOOLS: Wet saw or grinder with a diamond-tipped blade.

CUTTING STONE TILES.

Use a wet saw. Natural stone sometimes breaks along existing fissure lines when you try to cut it. If this becomes a problem, cut the tile through only two-thirds of its thickness, then flip it over and finish the cut from the other side.

STONE CUTTER

The best tool for making neat rectangular cutouts is a small stone cutter equipped with a diamond-tipped blade. Rent or borrow one from the tile dealer or a rental store. (Tile setters often mount a diamond-tipped blade on an electric grinder.) After cutting in each direction, knock the cutout free, and use tile nippers and a rubbing stone to clean up the corners.

SET IN SILICONE CAULK.

It may not look professional, but many tile setters use this technique. After you have dry-set all the tiles and know exactly where each tile will go, lift up one or two tiles at a time and make squiggles of clear silicone caulk on the substrate. Set the tiles in it quickly but carefully.

SEAL IT FIRST.

Manufacturers recommend that some types of stone tiles be set with an expensive epoxy mortar. An alternative technique is to coat the back of the tiles with nonporous epoxy. Once the coating dries, the tiles can be set with regular thinset mortar.

FINISH THE EDGE.

You can buy special edging tiles for some types of stone, or you can install narrow strips on the edge and set the tiles on top of them. Have the exposed edges polished by the dealer, or polish them with a rubbing stone and brush on several coats of varnish or polyurethane.

GROUTING TILE

Grout is a thin mortar mixture used to fill the joints between tiles. It protects tile edges from nicks and cracks, and it helps keep water from working its way below the tile surface. The size and color of the grout joint can be as important to the finished appearance of a floor as the tile itself, so it pays to choose and apply the grout carefully. (See page 117 for more on grout selection.) Do not apply grout until the adhesive has set, which normally takes up to 24 hours. If you are tiling more than one surface, such as a bathroom floor and walls, set the tiles on all the surfaces before you begin grouting. Then grout the walls before the floor. For stronger and less permeable grout, mix the powder with a latex additive rather than water.

CAUTION

USING COLORED GROUT

If you are using colored grout, mix a small test batch. Let it dry so you can see the finished color. Also spread some of the grout on a scrap tile to see if it stains the tile surface. When including a color additive to grout, mix it in before adding liquid. Make note of the exact quantities of ingredients used so you can mix consistent colors from one batch to the next.

YOU'LL NEED

TIME: Several hours for a typical bathroom floor.

SKILLS: Mixing and spreading grout, shaping grout joints, cleaning up.

TOOLS: Bucket and trowel, or mortar mixer; awl; rubber gloves; grout float; sponge; joint shaper.

1 MIX BY HAND…

Measure the liquid and pour it into the bucket. Add the dry ingredients a little at a time. Stir carefully with a clean trowel or piece of wood. Add more dry ingredients as needed.

OR USE A MORTAR MIXER.

For preparing large amounts, use a mortar mixer attached to an electric drill. Set the blade in the mixture, then mix at a slow speed. Don't lift the blade out until it stops turning.

2 REMOVE SPACERS, CLEAN JOINTS.

Before you begin spreading grout, remove all of the spacers between tiles. An awl or another thin tool will make removal easier. Also remove any adhesive that was squeezed into the joints between tiles. A razor blade or grout saw will speed this process. Vacuum the joints, and put masking tape over all expansion joints, which will be caulked later.

3 APPLY THE GROUT.

For a floor, pour enough grout on the tiles to cover about 3 square feet. For a wall, scoop up a good-sized dollop with the float. Hold the grout float at about a 35-degree angle, and spread the grout diagonally across the tiles. Press the grout firmly and completely into the joints. Make two or three passes, working in a different direction for each pass.

Tilt the float up so it is nearly perpendicular to the surface, and wipe away excess grout. Move diagonally to the joints, to avoid digging into them with the float.

4 WIPE AWAY THE EXCESS.

When you finish grouting one area, use a dampened sponge to wipe the tiles. Use a circular motion. If the grout is hard to wipe from the tiles, you have waited too long. Take care that the joints are consistent in depth. Rinse the sponge often.

A GROUT BAG

A grout (or mortar) bag looks a bit like a pastry bag used for decorating cakes. It is useful for grouting joints that can't be reached with a trowel, or for particularly porous tiles that soak up grout more quickly than you can clean it off the surface. Use a tip on the grout bag no wider than the width of the joint. Fill the bag with grout, then place the tip in the joint. Move the bag as you squeeze grout into the joint. Grout the full length of joints rather than grouting around each tile. Let the grout harden a little, then shape the joints. Once the grout has set for 30 minutes or more, sweep the joints with a broom or stiff brush to remove the excess.

ALLOW FOR EXPANSION

Don't forget about the expansion joints. These joints at corners and edges must be filled with expandable caulk, which allows the surfaces to expand and contract without cracking or damaging the tiles. Use masking tape to keep grout out of the expansion joints. Some grout will still seep under the tape and into the joint. So when you finish grouting, remove the tape and clean out the grout. Or wait for it to dry, and cut it out with a grout saw or utility knife. Let the joint dry completely, and vacuum before caulking.

Grouting tile *(continued)*

5 SHAPE THE JOINTS.

After wiping the tiles, clean and shape the joints. Pull a barely dampened sponge along grout lines, removing high spots as you go. Some people like thick grout lines that are nearly flush with the surface of the tile; others prefer grout lines that recede. The important thing is that the lines be consistent. Buy an adjustable joint shaper, or use a toothbrush handle or a wood dowel. The shaper should be a bit wider than the joint.

6 FILL THE GAPS.

If you notice a gap or inadvertently pull grout out from a joint, fill it right away with grout. Wearing rubber gloves, press a small amount into the void, filling it completely. Then shape the joint and remove any excess grout.

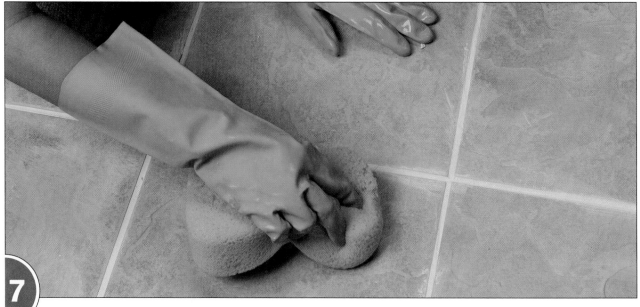

7 REMOVE THE GROUT FILM.

When you have cleaned the tile surfaces of grout and shaped the joints, let the grout set for another 15 or 20 minutes. With your sponge and a bucket of clean water, wearing rubber gloves, start the final cleaning of the tiles. Timing is critical: The grout should be dry enough to not be affected by the sponge, yet haze on the tile surface should not be so dry that it is difficult to remove. Rinse the sponge and wring it out. Pass the sponge slowly over a line of tiles. Flip the sponge over and make another straight run. Rinse the sponge and continue. With proper timing and careful execution, this process should remove nearly all of the grout residue from the tile surface. After another 15 minutes, polish the tiles with a dry piece of cheesecloth or a clean rag.

A key element to a successful tiling project is being able to seamlessly transition from one space to the next, room to room, creating a sense of consistency throughout the entire house. Rarely will you find that the surface in one room is exactly level with the next. The key to successfully tiling a transition—the area between your tile and another surface material—is foresight. You definitely want to plan your transitions when you lay out the project. The most common way to handle the transition area is to install a threshold. Thresholds can be made of wood, metal, or even marble and each is ideal for specific surfaces.

Choosing a threshold

Choose a threshold that will make the smoothest transition from one surface to the next. A tiled floor will more than likely be slightly higher than the adjoining floor. If you are working with an uneven surface, choose a threshold that has a recess on one side to accommodate the height difference. Wood thresholds are best for tile surfaces that butt up against wood. Choose a metal threshold if the tile lies next to carpet. (Metal thresholds are generally inexpensive and come in various shades of silver or bronze.) You can sometimes find marble thresholds that match your tile.

Installing a threshold

Whether you're installing wood, marble, or metal, first measure the space where the threshold will go. Next either purchase the threshold cut to size, or purchase one a bit larger than you need and cut it yourself. When installing a wood threshold, countersink the nailheads and fill the holes with matching wood putty for a clean, seamless look. If you choose a marble threshold, use the thinset mortar that you used to set the tile. To install a metal threshold, measure and cut the metal strip to size using a hacksaw. Pilot holes may or may not already be drilled into the metal strip. (If they aren't, measure the strip and drill evenly spaced pilot holes into the strip.) If they are, simply drive nails or screws through the holes into the floor. The joint between the threshold and the tile is considered an expansion joint and should be sealed with caulk rather than grout. See pages 119 and 148.

GREAT TRANSITIONS.

This great-room transitions from the living area to the dining area with a significant step. A wood threshold is used to make the transition. The wood is painted a light color that matches the room and also brings attention to the step, which helps guide guests unfamiliar with the space.

Maintenance
AND REPAIR

The key to preserving your tile is routine maintenance and care. If properly cared for, your tile will last for years, but naturally, over time, normal wear and tear will take its toll. Therefore, in addition to daily maintenance, knowing how to replace grout and tile is useful.

Maintenance begins with properly cleaning the tiles during and after installation (see page 149), sealing tiles and grout, wiping down kitchen and bath countertops daily with a sponge and warm water, and learning how to clean tough stains (use the "Removing Stains" chart on page 151 as a quick reference). Make sure you have the proper tools and materials on hand for maintaining your tiles, including a vacuum cleaner or broom, household cleaner, a bucket and sponge, and a tile sealer. When cleaning with a strong cleaner, remember to work in a well-ventilated room, and be sure to wear gloves and eye protection. Read the manufacturer's warning labels to prevent the combination of any toxic or hazardous materials, and do not mix bleach with other cleaners.

If your tiles require more than a good cleaning, or are in need of repair, the following pages will show you how to replace grout and tile. Often the grout is the first to show its age, and you can renew the look of your tile by refurbishing the grout. If a tile comes loose or is cracked, you will need to remove the old tile and replace it. In any case it is important to determine the root of the problem (substrate failure, for example) before proceeding with repairs. See pages 153 and 155 for step-by-step instructions on replacing grout and tiles.

SEALING GROUT

Tile is perfect for wet areas such as bathrooms. However caring for grout becomes even more important to prevent water from seeping behind the tiles. It is important to seal the grout after it has cured and reapply the sealer about every six months. See page 153 for tips on replacing grout.

TILE MAINTENANCE

If installed correctly, tile will last for years to come. If installing a shower with decorative tiles that fit together to create an overall design, such as the one featured, it will not be easy to find a replacement if a tile is damaged or broken. Take special care during installation and maintenance. You may want to consider buying extra tiles in case any become damaged. See page 149 for details on cleaning tile.

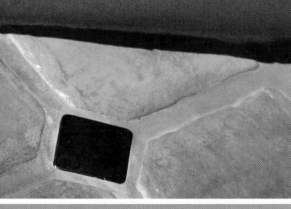

JOINT RENEWAL

Seasonal temperature changes can cause joint expansion between tile and other surfaces. Therefore a combination of an expandable foam and caulk are used to protect joints. This is especially important in outdoor areas where the surface may become wet. See page 152 for tips on caring for and repairing expansion joints.

STAIN REMOVAL

The impervious blue and white glazed tiles laid out in a staggered design provide a practical yet powerful look for this kitchen stove backsplash. Wipe down backsplashes routinely with warm water and a sponge. If you need to remove cooking grease or fat, clean with an all-purpose household cleaner. See page 151 for more on removing stains.

Caulk fills expansion joints around the perimeter of a tiled surface. Its flexibility allows adjacent surfaces to expand and contract without damaging tile; and it won't crack, as grout would. Many fine tile jobs have been marred by ugly caulking, so take the time to do it right. (See page 119 for information on choosing caulk.) Practice on scrap pieces until you feel you've got the knack. Place the tube in the gun, cut the tip, and puncture the seal with a long nail. Some people like to cut the tip at a severe angle; others like to cut it nearly straight across. Have a damp rag handy, soaked with water or mineral spirits, depending on the type of caulk you are using.

YOU'LL NEED

TIME: Less than 1 hour for most projects.

SKILLS: Applying and smoothing caulk, using a paint roller.

TOOLS: Caulk gun, paint roller and tray or paintbrush, rag.

GROUT SEALERS

You can significantly improve the durability of grout joints by sealing them. Wait until the grout has fully cured—a week or two—before applying grout sealer. Use a disposable foam-rubber paintbrush, which allows you to cover the grout without getting sealer on the tile. Allow the first coat to dry, then apply a second. Renew the grout sealer from time to time.

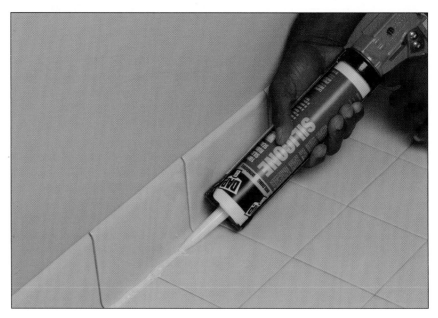

APPLY AND TOOL CAULK.

Position the tip of the tube on the surface to be caulked. Squeeze the trigger carefully until caulk begins to flow. Continue squeezing as you pull the gun along. Either leave the bead of caulk as it is, or use a finger or damp rag to smooth it. Strive for a consistent-looking line.

SEAL THE TILE.

Some tiles must be sealed when they are installed, or must have a sealer reapplied every few years. Check with the tile manufacturer for specific instructions. If you are installing unsealed tiles, you may have to apply the sealer before grouting. Otherwise renew the sealer as needed. A foam-cover paint roller works well for applying most types of tile sealer.

In addition to its beauty and durability, one of the big advantages of tile is that it is so easy to clean. If you attend to routine cleaning—wiping up spills that could stain right away, cleaning and sealing grout—you may only need to use the most common household products to keep your tile looking as good as new for years to come. Sweep and vacuum tile floors regularly. Use rugs or floor mats at entryways and other heavily traveled areas. On tiled countertops, use placemats and coasters under plates and glasses. If you must scrub a surface, avoid using metal scouring pads; woven-plastic scrubbers are much safer. And never mix different types of cleaning solutions, for example, chlorine bleach and ammonia.

Cleaning during installation

The first step to maintaining clean tiles is to make sure you clean properly during installation. After you apply the grout, wait approximately 15–20 minutes. Then take a damp sponge and wipe the tiles. Repeat this process.

Typically a slight grout haze will still be apparent on the tiles. To remove the haze, take a dry cloth and buff each tile.

Sealing grout and tiles

The second step to maintaining clean tiles is to apply a grout and tile sealant. The type of sealant you use depends on the type of tile you're working with. Check with your supplier to make sure you're choosing the right sealant. Wait a couple weeks before applying a sealant to make sure the grout has cured. All tiles and grout should be resealed about every six months.

ROUTINE CLEANING AND MAINTENANCE.

Wipe up spills immediately. Prepare a solution of warm water and dishwashing detergent or white vinegar, and thoroughly clean the tiled surface with a mop or sponge.

For stubborn dirt use an all-purpose soap-free household cleaner or a commercial tile cleaner. Rinse with clean water.

KEEP GROUT CLEAN.

Grout is the most demanding element of your tile floor. Coat the grout with a good-quality grout sealer after the grout has cured on a new installation. Reapply the sealer about every six months, or when the grout becomes porous and hard to clean. Before you reapply the sealer, you can allow some bleach to sit on the grout for a few minutes, and then use an old toothbrush to scrub clean.

Cleaning tile *(continued)*

Long-term maintenance

The key to long-term maintenance is in the daily cleaning of your tile, with bath and kitchen countertops and other high-traffic areas requiring the most attention. Wipe down your bath and kitchen countertops with a sponge and warm water daily. It's easy to just wipe the kitchen counter down when you're done cleaning up at the end of the day, and to wipe the bathroom counter down before going to bed. All you need is warm water—keep a special sponge underneath the sink for this purpose. And don't forget the backsplashes—they need daily attention as well. For floors, using a doormat at entrances from the outside can help cut down on dirt tracked into the house. Vacuum daily, and periodically use a mop with warm water as well. If you feel a stronger cleaner is required, simply add a touch of white vinegar to the water. If you're working on a tough stain, start with the mildest approach first. (See page 151 for a reference chart on removing stains.)

CLEANING STONE TILES.

Sweep and vacuum regularly. Wipe with a damp mop, warm water, and a little dishwashing detergent. Rinse thoroughly with clean water. Do not use abrasive, scented, or solvent-based cleaners.

CLEANING TUBS AND SHOWERS.

If routine cleaning doesn't remove soap and lime buildup, use a commercial bathroom cleaner or all-purpose cleaner. To remove caked-on dirt, leave the cleaner on the surface for a while before wiping it off. Prevent mildew by scrubbing grout joints with a solution of water and bleach. Also make sure the joints between your wall tiles and the tub edges are sealed with a silicone caulk. The caulk will shed water more easily, protecting your tub surround.

REMOVING STAINS

Glazed tile is highly stain-resistant; if it becomes discolored, then the glazing has failed. Unglazed tiles such as quarry tile and stone, however, can become badly stained. Prevention is the best remedy: Follow the cleaning tips on page 149, and perhaps even apply a coat of acrylic finish to a very porous tile surface that is liable to receive stains.

Often the best way to clean stains on tile is to make a paste of scouring powder and water. A thick paste will scour better than regular cleaner, and if you let it sit on the stain for several hours, it will continue to soak up unwanted color. On greasy stains a paste made of kitty litter and water can also work.

Though tile is strong and hard, take care not to scratch its surface. Use nylon scrubbers rather than steel wool, and take care when scraping with a metal tool.

REMOVE MILDEW.

Use a toothbrush dipped in household chlorine bleach to remove mildew stains. To remove the chlorine odor, wipe with a solution of baking soda and water.

RESERVE ACID CLEANERS.

Use acid cleaners only as a last resort to remove stains or grout haze. Muriatic acid is the most common. Start with a weak solution and increase the strength if that doesn't work. Always add acid to water, not the other way around. Protect your eyes and skin and wear a charcoal-filter mask; provide ventilation.

CAUTION

PROTECT YOURSELF AGAINST CHEMICALS

Many sealers, strippers, and cleaners are caustic, so exercise caution when using them. Read and follow the instructions on the label. Wear rubber gloves and eye protection, and provide sufficient ventilation so you don't have to inhale the fumes. Wear old clothes—they might get bleach stains or even develop holes. Use these products when children are out of the house, or at least when they can be kept a safe distance away.

REMOVING STAINS

Coffee, tea, blood, mustard, wine, fruit juice, rust, lipstick
Mix baking soda with a little water to create a thick paste. Rub the paste on the stain, and leave it until dry. Rinse and wipe dry. For deep, stubborn stains, apply full-strength household chlorine bleach. As a last resort, use an acid-based cleaner as directed on the label.

Oil, grease, tar
To remove oily stains from pavers, brick, or tiles made from concrete, prepare a liquid mixture of plaster of Paris. Brush the mixture on the stain and let it rest for 24 hours. Brush off and rinse. Repeat if necessary. Or use a commercial concrete or driveway cleaner.

Paint
Wipe a commercial paint remover on the paint, then carefully scrape off the paint with a razor knife.

Mineral deposits
Wipe with white vinegar or mix a solution of half water and half ammonia. Rinse and pat dry.

Cooking fats and grease
Clean with a concentrated solution of all-purpose household cleaner.

An expansion joint is the joint between the tiled area and another surface, such as the floor and the wall, or the counter and a backsplash. Due to expansion caused by seasonal temperature changes, these joints need special care. Rather than using grout, which hardens and will eventually crack, it is best to use a combination of backer rod (expandable foam) and caulk. A ¼-inch gap should be left between the tiled area and the other surface.

A crucial aspect of making your tile last is maintenance. Naturally, over time, tiles will need to be repaired. It's especially important to keep joints around wet areas, such as tub surrounds and kitchen and bath countertops, properly sealed. If too much water seeps through the joints, it can cause damage to the subsurface, requiring a lot more time and money to repair.

RECOGNIZING DAMAGE

To prevent further damage, it is important to be able to recognize when an expansion joint needs to be repaired. Signs to look for include cracks or holes in the caulking and mildew in the surrounding areas. (This may be a sign of water seeping through the cracks.)

YOU'LL NEED

TIME: About 1 hour, depending on the number of joints needing repair.

SKILLS: Working with backer rod and caulk.

TOOLS: Needle-nose pliers, putty knife, caulking tools.

1 REMOVE CAULK.

It's important to remove all of the old material and start with a clean and dry area. Using needle-nose pliers, remove the old caulk and backer rod. If there is already water damage, repair any damage before proceeding.

2 INSERT FOAM BACKER ROD.

Backer rod is an expandable foam material that allows the joint and caulk to compress and expand as surfaces shift. Make sure that the surface is clean and dry. Using a putty knife insert a new piece of backer rod, leaving ⅛ inch between the backer rod and the top of the tiled surface for the caulk.

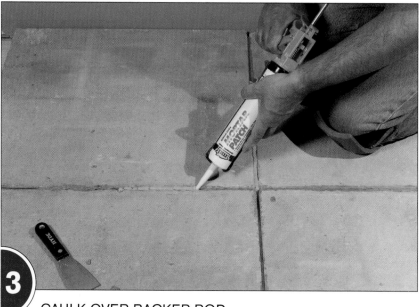

3 CAULK OVER BACKER ROD.

Next apply a generous line of caulk over the backer rod to form a flexible seal. Caulking compounds do vary. Depending on the space, you may want to apply a mildew-resistant caulk. See page 148 for more information on applying caulk.

REPLACING GROUP

Before you start repairing grout joints, try to determine the source of the problem. Loose or cracked grout over a fairly large area may indicate a structural problem below the surface; a few gaps or cracks may be due to a sloppy grouting job in that area. If the grout has been in bad shape for some time, you should try to determine if water has managed to pass through the substrate, which can cause tiles to buckle and may even lead to structural problems.

YOU'LL NEED

TIME: A couple of hours for spot repairs, 1–2 days for a large regrouting job.

SKILLS: Sawing or digging out old grout carefully, grouting.

TOOLS: Grout saw, grout float, utility knife, grout bag, sponge, bucket, dry cloth.

1 REMOVE OLD GROUT.

Remove grout with a utility knife or an old hacksaw blade. For very narrow joints, use the tip of an awl. If you have to remove a lot of grout, the job will go much faster with a grout saw (available at tile dealers and large home centers), a small handheld tile saw, or an angle grinder equipped with a diamond-tipped blade (see page 111). Vacuum the joints and clean the tiles to remove dirt, oil, or soap scum.

2 APPLY NEW GROUT.

Unless you are regrouting the entire installation, try to match the color of the new grout with the old. (Take a loose piece of grout with you when you go shopping.) If you have doubts about the color, mix a small amount and let it dry. After 2 or 3 days, compare the colors. Mix the grout with a latex additive before applying. The additive will waterproof and help prevent cracks in the future. Apply small amounts of grout with a grout bag or your finger.

3 CLEAN AND SEAL.

Clean the grout using a dampened sponge to wipe the tiles. Wipe with a circular motion, making sure the grout joints are consistent in depth. Rinse your sponge often. Let the grout dry for several days before applying a grout sealer.

REMOVING TILE

Whether you're removing one cracked tile or an entire wall or floor of tiles, it's important to go about the project with the proper tools and patience, so as not to cause more damage. Before you remove the tile, it's best to determine what type of adhesive was used for the initial installation. If organic mastic was used, the tile will be much easier to remove; a thinset mortar will require a bit more work. After removing tile, if you find the substrate or drywall is weakened or damaged, you will want to strengthen it before applying a new tile. Remove all the tiles necessary to repair the damage underneath.

YOU'LL NEED

TIME: A couple hours to remove one or two tiles, 1–2 days to remove an entire floor or wall.

SKILLS: Testing the strength of a wall or floor, using a drill.

TOOLS: Drill, grout saw, hammer, cold chisel, putty knife, screwdriver.

REPLACING TILES

It's unlikely that you have extra tile laying around from the original installation job; therefore, you will need to find replacement tile that will match. One manufacturer's tile may not be like another's, so you may have a challenge. Start by seeing if the name of the manufacturer is written on the back of the tile. If it is you can narrow your field pretty quickly. If not take the old tile to your supplier; they will help you find a tile that will match. And don't forget about matching up the grout. Cleaning the old grout will help you match up a new grout more effectively.

1 REMOVE GROUT.

It will be much easier to remove the tile, and there will be less chance of damaging surrounding tiles, if the grout around the tile is removed first. Use a grout saw to loosen the grout around the tile. Then you can use a screwdriver to remove the excess grout.

2 SCORE THE TILE.

If the tile is already loose, you may be able to simply pry it off with a cold chisel or putty knife. If it still adheres tightly to the wall, use a drill with a carbide-tipped hole saw and drill several holes over the surface of the tile. This will weaken the tile and make it easier for you to break off. Be sure to wear protective eyewear.

3 STRIKE THE CENTER.

Using a cold chisel and hammer, strike the center of the tile gently. Hold the chisel carefully—you want to avoid coming into contact with, and potentially damaging, the surface underneath.

4 REMOVE BROKEN TILE.

Using a putty knife gently remove the cracked tile, being careful not to damage the surrounding tiles. If you find that any surrounding tiles begin to crack, it is an indication that there is greater damage underneath the surface. Remove as many tiles as needed to repair the surface before continuing. You will want to remove any old adhesive before setting the new tile.

REPLACING TILE

If a number of tiles have come loose, your main job may be to repair a substrate that has been water damaged. Remove as many tiles as necessary so you can firm up any soft parts of the substrate; patch with backerboard. If you are working near a tub or sink, be sure to cover the tub, especially the drain to prevent scratches and a clogged drain.

It may be difficult to find a replacement tile. If you don't have any spare tiles left from the original installation, take a piece with you to the store and find tiles that match in size and color.

YOU'LL NEED

TIME: 1–2 hours to replace a tile.

SKILLS: Handling a chisel and hammer, setting tile.

TOOLS: Hammer, beater block, cold chisel, putty knife.

1 **REMOVE OLD TILE.**

If the tile doesn't simply pop out, break its connection to adjacent tiles by sawing through the grout joints around the tile. With a hammer, tap the damaged tile to crack it into smaller pieces. Don't hit too hard; you could damage the substrate or shake other tiles loose. Use a cold chisel with the hammer to chip away the pieces. Be sure to wear eye protection.

2 **PREPARE THE SURFACE.**

Use a putty knife or margin trowel to scrape away all of the old adhesive. Remove any remaining grout from the joints. Create a smooth, clean surface for the new tile.

3 **INSTALL NEW TILE.**

Use the same adhesive used on the original installation. If you don't know what it was, use an adhesive appropriate to the installation (see page 115). Spread a thin coat of the adhesive over the entire back of the replacement tile. Spread another coat on the setting bed. Press the tile into

place, giving it a gentle twist. Use a beater block and hammer to set the tile flush. If necessary hold the tile in place with masking tape. Wait one or two days before grouting, then wait several more days and seal the grout (see page 119).

GLOSSARY

For words not listed here or for more about those that are, refer to the index, pages 158–160.

Actual dimension. The true size of a tile. *See* nominal dimension.

Backerboard. A ready-made surface for setting tile. Also called cement board. Can be cement-based or gypsum-based.

Backsplash. Typically a 3- to 4-inch-high length of material at the back edge of a countertop extending the full length.

Batten. A piece of wood used to secure a joint or to support tiles while they cure.

Beater block. Used to press tiles evenly into adhesive. Can be a store-bought rubber-faced model or a piece of plywood that you've covered with terry cloth.

Building codes. Community ordinances governing the manner in which a home or other structure may be constructed or modified. Most codes deal primarily with fire and health concerns and have separate sections relating to electrical, plumbing, and structural work.

Bullnose tiles. Tiles shaped to define the edges of an installation. Also called caps.

Butt joint. The joint formed by two pieces of material when fastened end to end, end to face, or end to edge.

Buttering. Applying mortar on bricks or blocks with a trowel before laying them.

Casing. The trimming around a door, window, or other opening.

Caulk. Any one of a variety of compounds used to seal seams and joints against infiltration of water and air.

Cement board. A backerboard with a mesh coat. Cement board is a surface for setting tile.

Ceramic tile. Made from refined clay usually mixed with additives and water and hardened in a kiln. Can be glazed or unglazed.

Darby. A long-bladed wood float commonly used to smooth the surface of freshly poured concrete in situations where using a smaller float isn't practical.

Dobie. Small blocks used to support rebar or wire mesh in concrete.

Drywall. A basic interior building material consisting of big sheets of pressed gypsum faced with heavy paper on both sides. Also known as gypsum board, plasterboard, and Sheetrock (a brand name). Moisture-resistant drywall is known as greenboard or blueboard.

Expansion joint. The space built into a structure between it and an existing structure to allow materials to expand and contract during temperature changes without damage to the surface.

Field tiles. Flat tiles with nonrounded edges used on the main portion of an installation.

Float. A rectangular wood or metal hand tool used for smoothing and compressing wet concrete.

Glazing. A protective and decorative coating, often colored, that is fired onto the surface of some tiles.

Granite. A quartz-based stone with a tough, glossy appearance; granite is harder than marble.

Greenboard. Similar to regular drywall, this material is moisture resistant, though not waterproof. Also referred to as blueboard.

Grout. A thin mortar mixture used to fill the joints between tiles. (*See* mortar.)

Grout float. A rubber-backed trowel used for pressing the grout into the joints.

Impervious tile. Tiles least likely to absorb water, generally used in hospitals, restaurants, and other commercial locations.

Inside corner. The point at which two walls form an internal angle, as in the corner of a room.

Isolation membrane. A subsurface layer for tile installations. Chlorinated polyethylene (CPE) sheets are used for an isolation membrane.

Jamb. The top and side frames of a door or window opening.

Joint compound. A synthetic formula used in combination with paper tape to conceal joints between drywall panels.

Ledger. A piece of wood used to secure a joint or to support tiles while they set.

Level. When any surface is at true horizontal. Also a tool used to determine level.

Marble. A hard and durable limestone characterized by varied patterns and colors of veins.

Masonry cement. A special mix of portland cement and hydrated lime used for preparing mortar. The lime adds to the workability of the mortar.

Membrane. A subsurface layer for tile installations. Tar paper is used for a waterproofing membrane. Chlorinated polyethylene (CPE) sheets are used for an isolation membrane.

Mexican paver. Unglazed tile most often used on floors.

Mortar. A mixture of masonry cement, masonry sand, and water. For most jobs the proportion of cement to sand is 1:3. Also the process of applying mortar.

Mosaic tile. Small (1- or 2-inch) vitreous squares or hexagons, mounted on sheets or joined with adhesive strips.

Nominal dimension. The stated size of a tile, which usually includes a standard grout joint. The actual dimension is somewhat smaller.

Nonvitreous tile. Porous ceramic tiles that should be used indoors in dry locations.

Organic mastic. A premixed setting adhesive for tiles. Used often on walls because it holds tiles in place without slippage.

Outside corner. The point at which two walls form an external angle; the corner you can usually walk around.

Particleboard. Panels made from compressed wood chips and glue.

Pavers. Vitreous floor tiles, usually ⅜ inch thick and glazed or unglazed.

Plumb. When a surface is at true vertical.

Plumb bob. Weight used with a plumb line to align vertical points and determine plumb.

Quarry tile. Unglazed, vitreous tiles, usually ½-inch thick, used on floors.

Rod saw. A strip of tungsten carbide that fits into a standard hacksaw body, used for cutting tight curves in tile.

Screed. A straightedge, often a 2×4 or 2×6, used for leveling concrete as it is poured into a form.

Sealant. Coatings used to protect tile and grout from water infiltration.

Semivitreous tile. Semiporous ceramic tiles that can be used indoors, in dry to occasionally wet locations.

Shower pan. The floor of a shower stall, which houses the drain. Can be a prefabricated unit made of fiberglass, acrylic, terrazzo, or other materials.

Slate. A rough-surfaced tile split, rather than sliced, from quarried stone.

Snap cutter. Cutting tool for tile. Resembles a glass cutter, except that it is mounted on a guide bar.

Spacers. Small pieces of plastic used to ensure consistent grout-joint width between tiles.

Square. The condition that exists when one surface is at a 90-degree angle to another. Also a tool used to determine square.

Stone tile. Marble, granite, flagstone, and slate. Dimensioned (or gauged) stone is cut to uniform size. Hand-split stone (or cleft stone) varies in size.

Straightedge. An improvised tool, usually a 1×4 or 2×4 with a straight edge, used to mark a straight line on material or to determine if a surface is even.

Subfloor. Usually plywood or another sheet material covering the floor joists.

Substrate. The setting bed and any other layers beneath a tile surface.

Taping. The process of covering drywall joints with tape and joint compound.

Terrazzo tiles. Small pieces of granite or marble set in mortar, then polished.

Thinset mortar. A setting adhesive for tiles.

Tile nippers. Cutting tool for making small notches and curves in tile. Resemble pliers but have carbide-tipped edges.

Toenail. To drive a nail at an angle to hold together two pieces of material.

Trim tile. Tiles shaped to turn corners or define the edges of an installation. Includes cove trim, bullnose, V-cap, quarter-round, inside corner, and outside corner.

Trowel. Any of several flat and oblong or pointed metal tools used for handling adhesive and grout and/or concrete and mortar.

Vitreous tile. Ceramic tiles with a low porosity, used indoors or outdoors, in wet or dry locations.

Wet saw. A power tool for cutting tile. A pump sprays water to cool the diamond-tipped blade and remove chips.

INDEX

Index *(continued)*

METRIC CONVERSIONS

U.S. Units to Metric Equivalents			Metric Units to U.S. Equivalents		
To convert from	Multiply by	To Get	To convert from	Multiply by	To Get
Inches	25.4	Millimeters	Millimeters	0.0394	Inches
Inches	2.54	Centimeters	Centimeters	0.3937	Inches
Feet	30.48	Centimeters	Centimeters	0.0328	Feet
Feet	.03048	Meters	Meters	3.2808	Feet
Yards	.9144	Meters	Meters	1.0936	Yards
Miles	1.6093	Kilometers	Kilometers	0.6214	Miles
Square inches	6.4516	Square centimeters	Square centimeters	0.1550	Square inches
Square feet	0.0929	Square meters	Square meters	10.764	Square feet
Square yards	0.8361	Square meters	Square meters	1.1960	Square yards
Acres	0.4047	Hectares	Hectares	2.4711	Acres
Square miles	2.5899	Square kilometers	Square kilometers	0.3861	Square miles
Cubic inches	16.387	Cubic centimeters	Cubic centimeters	0.0610	Cubic inches
Cubic feet	0.0283	Cubic meters	Cubic meters	35.315	Cubic feet
Cubic feet	28.316	Liters	Liters	0.0353	Cubic feet
Cubic yards	0.7646	Cubic meters	Cubic meters	1.038U	Cubic yards
Cubic yards	764.55	Liters	Liters	0.0013	Cubic yards

To convert from degrees Fahrenheit (F) to degrees Celsius (C), first subtract 32, then multiply by ⅚.

To convert from degrees Celsius to degrees Fahrenheit, multiply by ⅚, then add 32.